W9-BZA-346

ONIONS

A COUNTRY GARDEN COOKBOOK

ONIONS

A COUNTRY GARDEN COOKBOOK

By Jesse Ziff Cool

Photography by Deborah Jones

CollinsPublishersSanFrancisco

A Division of HarperCollinsPublishers

For my mother, June Ziff,
who is the kind of mom every human being deserves and who
taught me that earthiness and elegance go hand in hand.

First published in USA 1995 by Collins Publishers San Francisco
Copyright © 1995 by Collins Publishers San Francisco
Recipe and text copyright © 1995 Jesse Ziff Cool
Photographs copyright © 1995 Deborah Jones
Food Stylist: Sandra Cook
Floral and Prop Stylist: Sara Slavin
Art Direction and Design: Jennifer Barry
Series Editor: Meesha Halm
Illustrations copyright © Maryjo Koch
Library of Congress Cataloging-in-Publication Data
Cool, Jesse Ziff.
Onions: a country garden cookbook/by Jesse Ziff Cool:
photography by Deborah Jones.
p.   cm.
Includes index.
ISBN 0-00-255452-6
1. Cookery (Onions)   I. Title.
TX803.05C66 1995
641.6'525—dc20   CIP 94-29407

All rights reserved, including the right of reproduction in whole
or in part or in any form.

Printed in China
1 3 5 7 9 10 8 6 4 2

Acknowledgments

The onion family is not a simple one. I learned more than I ever dreamed of from allium experts around the country. When I got lost in my monthly subscription to Onion World magazine instead of a lusty novel, my farmer sweetheart began to question how far I was buried in the roots of the onion world.

My thanks go to many knowledgeable people, who include Ros Creasy, my gardening guru; Wendy Krupnick, garden goddess and good friend; Paul and Dru of Full Belly Farms, who have filled my belly with the best organically grown onions year after year; Greenswald Nursery for information on onion sprouting; Nancy Teksten of the National Onion Association, for her endless support and encouraging words; Ian Lockhart, Bob Scater, Ron Voss, Rick Watson, Bill Sherman and Ron Marchini for direction; Paula Foucheck and Betty Ricks of Tex Fresh, for talking onions with me; Bonnie Yuill-Thornton of Dragon Fly Farm, for letting the photography team go wild in their garden; and Gale Kinsey, Eric Toshalis and Sheri Kalbaugh, for their inspirational recipes.

Thanks also to Darren Dunbar, for joyfully testing the recipes. And, as always, my appreciation goes to the gang at Flea St. Café, for exuding pride in the restaurant and putting into practice its philosophy of eating seasonally and organically.

Collins Publishers has surrounded me with care and support, and my greatest gratitude goes to my editor, Meesha Halm, who never loses patience. My thanks also to Dayna Macy, Maura Carey Damacion and the founding mother of the Country Garden Cookbook series, Jenny Barry. Also my most esteemed gratitude to my talented buddy Deborah Jones and fantastic food stylist Sandra Cook, for creating photographs that depict onions as they really are—earthy, glorious and breathtaking!

My appreciation goes to Lisa Fenwick, Linda Krain, David Gorn, Diarmuid McGuire, Eric Mason and especially Stuart Dickson, all of who eat my food, encourage my writing and push me through the tough spots. Finally, I want to thank my two boys, Jonah and Joshua, and my father, Eddie, all of whom are beautiful and healthy, proving the value of eating lots of onions and garlic.

Collins and the photography team would also like to thank Jeri Jones and Helga Sigvaldadottir, photo assistants; Allyson Levy, food styling assistant; Kristen Wurtz, design and production coordinator; Jonathan Mills, production manager; and Assumpta Curry, production. Thanks also to Melanie Fife and to Dragon Fly Farm in Healdsburg, California, for the delicious onions. Finally, to garden designer Michael Bates and his wife Helen, for allowing the photography to be shot on location at his garden on Sonoma Mountain in Glen Ellen, California.

CONTENTS

INTRODUCTION

I have always believed that onions and garlic run through my blood. My heritage is Jewish and Italian, and these twin influences taught me early on that onions and garlic are as important as salt, pepper and a close-knit family. Nana taught me how to prepare old-fashioned Italian food rich with these ingredients. I remember staying close to her in the kitchen while she cooked greens laced with olive oil and stuffed huge ravioli with slowly stewed onions and meat. Bubbe cooked strictly kosher, feeding me oniony potato pancakes and garlicky homemade pickles. Both house-holds greeted me at the front door with the welcome aromas of onions or garlic drifting from the kitchen. To this day, the fragrances from a pan of sautéing onions or the drifting perfume of garlic roasting in the oven draw me back into the past.

At an early age, I was taught that eating lots of garlic would bring me good luck and that onions were essential to the maintenance of healthy blood. It is therefore no surprise to me that the members of my family rarely get sick, and that when they do, the illness is always short-lived. Call it heredity, I believe it's the onions and garlic.

I have had a lifelong love affair with root vegetables, and those of the *Allium* genus, which includes onions, leeks, shallots, garlic and chives, are without question the root vegetables I crave most. Unsung heroes of the kitchen, the onion and its versatile kin can take an understated dish and turn it into a culinary event to remember.

One of the world's oldest cultivated vegetables, the onion is part of the large and varied lily family. It has traveled through time, intimately woven into history since its existence was first recorded in a Sumerian text some four thousand years ago. Its origin is reputed to be somewhere in southwest Asia, from where it was carried by explorers to all corners of the world. Today, wild onion grasses can still be found in Europe, North America and Asia.

The onion clan holds a profound place in folklore. In Greece and Italy, to this day, garlic is believed to be capable of warding off the devil, and at the same time, it is coveted as an aphrodisiac and a token of good luck. Leeks, native to the Far East and a symbol of long life and fortitude, found their way to the British Isles, where they became a standard cooking ingredient as well as the national symbol of Wales.

These days, the onion's first cousins—leeks, shallots and chives—are gaining recognition as more than just seasonings, and many of the recipes in this book exemplify that fact.

Garlic is the wild child of the family, passionate and beloved, and capable of flavoring our food with gusto. All the members of the onion clan can be prepared in countless ways. They can be eaten raw during peak season and roasted, boiled, sautéed, deep-fried, braised, grilled or pickled anytime of the year. What other vegetables boast such versatility?

Take advantage of the fact that onions are a seasonal vegetable. There are two different kinds of onion, those that are harvested in the spring and summer and those that are harvested in the fall. The differences between these two types of onions are crucial. Spring/summer onions are mild, full of water, fragile, and best eaten raw or lightly cooked. Fall/storage onions are more pungent, dense and meaty, and best cooked. Using the right onion can make a difference in the depth or gentleness of flavor that the cook is able to achieve.

However, don't limit the members of the onion family to specifically defined culinary roles. When a dish calls for green onions, try substituting chives, baby leeks, green garlic or young shallot shoots. In recipes where onions are sautéed, use shallots or leeks for a softer, gentler flavor. Substitute red onions for yellow and leeks for mild white onions. And remember, onions are more than just bulbs: Use them throughout their lives, from sprouts to greens to mature bulbs.

GLOSSARY

Selecting and Storing:

Bulbing Onions:

Fall/Storage Onions: Choose heavy onions with no sign of mold or rot. Outer skins should be crisp and papery. Smell the onion: There should be little or no strong odor. Avoid onions that have sprouted; this indicates that they have been stored too long. They can be kept in a cool, dry place for months.

Spring/Summer Onions: Select heavy, firm onions without cracks, bruises, indentations or signs of mold or mildew. Because of their high water content and low sulfuric compounds, they bruise easily and are highly perishable. Refrigerate for up to a week. Often sold at produce stands carefully packaged in netting or Styrofoam trays.

Green Onions: Choose green onions with crisp outer leaves and fresh-looking roots. Avoid those that are slimy or rubbery. Some will be shaped like crescent moons; others will be round and hollow. Refrigerate wrapped in a moist towel or in a plastic bag for up to 5 days.

Pearl Onions: Select firm, tight bulbs that, for their size, are heavy and full of water. Refrigerate for up to a month.

Chives: Choose onion and garlic chives that are still moist at the base. Onion chives should not be limp. Garlic chives are softer and may be more flexible, but should feel full of moisture and never be withered. All chives should smell of either onion or garlic. Refrigerate in a glass of cold water, wrapped in a damp kitchen towel or slipped into a plastic bag.

Garlic: Select garlic with firm, plump bulbs; press the cloves to ensure that they have not dried out. The papery outer skin should be crisp and there should be no sign of mold. Choose large heads for ease of preparation and roasting, but realize that freshness and variety, not size, are indications of flavor. Garlic bulbs, because of their natural oils, must be stored in a cool, dark, dry place. They must not touch other moist vegetables, or they will deteriorate quickly and transfer their strong flavor to absorbent neighbors. Hang bulbs in braids or place in a well-ventilated basket.

Green garlic is young garlic before it begins to form cloves or a papery covering. Choose green garlic that has firm white- or red-streaked stalks and crisp green leaves. It should not be rubbery. Refrigerate as you would green onions, in a sealed plastic bag or moist kitchen towel.

Leeks: Leeks should have moist, white roots. Any browning or softening is most likely an indication of age. The leaves and roots should be free of cracks, with no yellowing, browning or wilting. Choose small leeks; the large ones may be tough and stringy. Do not wash leeks before storing. Wipe or rinse the outside only and refrigerate wrapped in a moist kitchen towel or in a sealable plastic bag or container for up to a week.

Shallots: Choose shallots that are firm and plump with dry roots and skins. Avoid sprouted shallots, as sprouting indicates age. Store shallots in a cool, dark, dry place in a paper bag.

Preparing and Cooking:

Onions: Onions contain the enzyme alliinase, which, when exposed to air, combines with the onions' sulfuric compounds. This chemical reaction irritates our eyes and causes tearing. To avoid the burning and crying, chill onions for at least 30 minutes before cutting them. Or place a cutting board in the sink and peel and cut the onion while the tap water is running over it. When cutting bulb onions, start by slicing off the top, then peel back the skin of the outer layers, leaving the root intact. Since the root has the largest concentration of sulfuric compounds, leaving it whole can save you a lot of grief. If all else fails, wear a pair of tight swimming goggles while cutting onions, causing a few giggles instead of tears.

You can control the strength of an onion's flavor in a variety of ways. The first thing to remember is that the more pungent the onion is raw, the sweeter it becomes when cooked. To reduce the sharpness of onions before cooking, soak them in water or milk for about 15 minutes. Cut onions as close to cooking or serving time as possible, because the flavor and aroma intensify over time. When cooking onions, whether sautéing them slowly on the stove top or roasting them in the oven, use low or medium heat. Intense heat makes strong-flavored onions bitter. On the other hand, deep-frying or searing onions over high heat for a short amount of time maintains their true flavor. If you plan to serve onions raw, marinate them in vinegar for 30 minutes. Or pour boiling water over sliced onions, then drain immediately. The crunch will remain, but the sharpness will be gone.

To reduce the amount of oil or other fat needed for sautéing onions, select a heavy-bottomed pan and use only a small amount of oil (1 tablespoon per 1 1/2 pounds onions). Place the pan with the oil over very low heat, add the onions and coat them well. Cook the onions, adding a small amount of stock or water when necessary to keep them from sticking. The moisture in the onions will be released, creating natural sweet juices.

Home-dried onions are far superior to the ones you can buy at the store. They are typically sweeter and more concentrated. Dried onions impart a unique sweet, deep flavor to soups or stews. Or chop them and use as an interesting garnish for salads.

When drying onions, use the sweetest, most pungent onions available for the most flavorful results. To dry onions in the oven, peel and then cut into slices 1/4 inch thick. Arrange on a rack on a baking sheet or roasting pan and place in an oven preheated to 150 degrees F. Store airtight for approximately 3 hours, or until the onions are nearly brittle.

Garlic: Fresh garlic is best for cooking. Dried or powdered garlic is bitter and has an aftertaste. After the mechanics of peeling and chopping are mastered, there is never any need to use dehydrated garlic again.

To remove the cloves from a garlic bulb, place the bulb on a flat work surface, pointed side down, and gently push on the whole bulb, moving it from side to side, until the bulb loosens and the cloves, still in their skins, separate.

To peel cloves but still keep them intact, immerse the cloves in boiling water for 1 minute, then immediately immerse in cold water. The skins should slip off easily. To peel cloves for crushing or chopping, place a clove on a

work surface and, using the flat side of a large cleaver or chef's knife, push down on the clove, crushing it. Remove the skin.

The flavor of garlic changes depending on how it is prepared. The finer it is chopped, the stronger the flavor. The sulfur compounds in the cloves create the strong garlic taste; with more thorough chopping, more compounds are activated. The strongest, hottest part of the clove is the tiny green sprout at its center. Some people remove this before chopping to eliminate any sharp, bitter flavor.

I rarely use a garlic press, although it is a quick and easy way to crush cloves almost to a purée. The advantage of a garlic press is that there is no real need to peel the garlic first. Just put the clove, skin and all, in the press and squeeze. The pulp will go through the holes. Then pull up the handle and remove the flattened skin. Some cooks disdain the use of garlic presses, insisting that the result is overly pungent rather than pleasantly potent.

To store peeled, whole or chopped raw garlic cloves, place in an empty jar, cap tightly and refrigerate for up to a few days. Although many people prefer to store garlic in olive oil, the Food and Drug Administration recommends that home cooks throw such mixtures out after a day, even if stored in the refrigerator, to prevent botulism.

Sautéing garlic is the way to get the most flavor with the least bite. Be sure to heat the oil or butter first, then reduce the heat before adding the garlic. Garlic burns easily and high heat can make it bitter and unpleasant. Cooking garlic slowly over low heat destroys the odoriferous compound, diallyl disulfide, and softens both its smell and its flavor. Cooked whole cloves carry the mildest flavor. Boiled whole cloves, which have a mild, potatolike flavor and consistency, make a delicate, low-fat seasoning. Steamed garlic is also very mild and has a similar texture and flavor to boiled garlic without the loss of vitamins and minerals in the cooking water.

Whole roasted garlic has a soft, sweet, almost nutty flavor. For roasting directions, see pages 28 and 30.

Green Onions: Green onions—both the white bottoms and the green tops—are excellent raw and cooked. Clean and trim tops.

Pearl Onions: To peel pearl onions, cut off the root ends and drop the onions into a pot of boiling water for a minute or two, or until the skin peels away easily.

Chives: Chives are primarily used as an herbal seasoning. They complement many foods, including scrambled eggs, goat cheese, roasted vegetables and grilled fish. Lavender chive blossoms impart a discreet onion flavor. In addition to using chives as a seasoning or garnish, dip whole chives, including blossoms, in tempura batter and deep-fry them. Or use chives to tie together bundles of asparagus or other vegetables.

Leeks: Young leeks are typically clean and can be lightly rinsed. Medium-sized and large leeks must be washed thoroughly to remove all dirt or grime. To clean, peel away damaged or tough outer leaves. Cut off the tough, inedible greens (and freeze, if you like, to use for making stock). Slit the leek lengthwise, but cut only halfway through, stopping at the center. Place in water to cover and soak for 15 minutes. If you are short on time, split the leek lengthwise and place under running water to remove dirt. If the leek's layers are full of dirt and you intend to slice the leek for cooking, cut it before soaking the slices in water, changing the water and rinsing until all dirt is removed.

Leeks double as both a vegetable and a seasoning. Whether boiled, steamed, roasted or grilled with a dash of salt and pepper or cloaked in a rich cream sauce, leeks are a perfect side dish. Cooked and puréed into a soup or mashed with potatoes, they perform as a wonderful seasoning. Leeks also impart a light, aromatic onion flavor to stocks.

Treat baby leeks as you would young garlic or onions. Slice thinly and toss raw on salads and egg dishes or into steaming bowls of soup or pasta. Or marinate and grill over hot coals as a tasty finishing touch to any barbecue.

Shallots: When cooked, the flesh of shallots softens faster than that of an onion, making them particularly popular in the preparation of sauces and stews. They can also be braised, roasted, boiled or creamed whole as you would pearl onions.

Try coating a handful of shallots, skins intact, with olive oil, threading them onto skewers, and then placing them on the grill for 10 minutes. Or, if you have a smoker, add whole shallots while your fish or poultry is smoking.

Nutritional and Health Benefits: For thousands of years, the *Allium* genus has been held in high regard for its strengthening and restorative properties. But until recently, belief in these healing qualities was confined to folklore and homeopathic circles. Today, however, a number of chemicals found naturally in onions, in particular allicin, have been scientifically proven to aid in both the prevention and the treatment of various blood disorders.

Onions, shallots, leeks, chives and garlic, when included as a regular part of the diet, can minimize heart and circulatory system problems by reducing cholesterol levels in the blood. The National Cancer Institute has incorporated all the members of the onion family into its list of cruciferous vegetables, calling them promising agents in combating, in particular, stomach cancer. More importantly, quercetin, an antioxidant present in the whole family, is recognized as a cancer-blocking compound by the National Institute of Health. Onions also have excellent antiseptic qualities, can loosen phlegm related to colds and asthma and will act as a diuretic. Putting an onion on a bee sting or cut will help soothe the pain and stop the bleeding.

Garlic is the wonder drug of the vegetable bin. When it comes to homeopathic prescriptions, it continues to be considered one of the most valuable aids for treating a wide range of maladies, from digestive problems to conditions of the lymph system. The National Cancer Institute has named garlic as one of the best natural cancer preventatives, and a recent cancer prevention study has reported that cancer patients who have ingested anywhere from three cloves to a whole bulb of fresh garlic a day have been able to keep their ailments in remission. Garlic is also considered a cold and asthma preventative.

Leeks are said to have medicinal properties similar to those of garlic. They reputedly reduce cholesterol, keep blood pressure low and aid in the prevention of cancer. Some recent studies have also shown leeks, along with other members of the onion family, to boost the immune system. For those who find garlic difficult to digest, leeks are a good alternative, as they are softer and milder, yet still offer the many benefits of garlic.

Controlling the Odors: To alleviate the halitosis that can occur after eating raw onions or garlic, eat fresh parsley or mint leaves; suck on lemon wedges or chew on orange, lime or lemon peel; or chew on a coffee bean or a piece of vanilla bean. To remove the scent of onions from your hands, rub with tomato juice, salt or lemon wedges. To clean kitchen equipment, rub work surfaces and equipment with salt, lemon or white vinegar. Remember, too, cooked onions and garlic cause fewer breath problems and are easier to digest.

Yellow Cooking

White Globe

Red Globe

Maui (Granex)

Walla Walla

Green Onion
(Scallion)

Sweet Spanish

Vidalia (Granex)

California Sweet Imperial (Grano)

Onion Sprouts

Texas Spring Sweet (Grano)

White Pearl

Purplette

Cipollini

Red Torpedo

Red Spring

Chives

Garlic Chives

Green Garlic

California Early Garlic

California Late Garlic

Elephant Garlic

Rocambole

Large American Flag Leek

Red Shallot

Yellow Shallot

Baby Leek

Measurements and Equivalents:

Bulbing Onions:

1 medium onion = 1 cup chopped or sliced or 2/3 cup grated

1 large onion = 1 1/2 cups chopped or sliced

1 pound onions = 4 cups chopped or sliced = 1 1/2 to
 2 cups cooked

Pearl Onions:

1 basket pearl onions (approximately 10 ounces) = 20 to 60
 onions, depending upon their size

1 cup unpeeled pearl onions = 10 to 25 onions, depending
 upon their size

Green Onions:

1 bunch green onions = 6 small or 4 large green onions

1 pound green onions = 2 1/2 cups trimmed and chopped

Garlic:

1 medium clove = approximately 1 teaspoon finely chopped

3 medium cloves = approximately 1 tablespoon finely chopped

Leeks:

2 pounds leeks = 1 pound cleaned (white part only) =
 approximately 4 cups chopped = 2 cups cooked

ONIONS *(Allium cepa):* All onions can be eaten throughout their growing season until they go to seed. From onion sprouts to tender shoots to small, young sweet bulbs and large mature bulbs, each stage of the onion's development has a role in the kitchen. Over 400 onion varieties are grown in the United States, many with names referring to their place of origin (Texas Spring Sweet, Stockton Red, Hawaiian Maui).

However, it is seasonality, rather than geographical source, that affects the character of onions, and this must be taken into consideration when selecting the onions and deciding how the onions are to be used in the kitchen.

Bulbing Onions: Often called globe onions because of their shape, bulbing onions are divided into two categories. Within each category, they come in a range of colors and sizes. Fall/storage onions, the variety with which most people are familiar, is considered the workhorse of the kitchen. However, spring/summer onions, often called sweet onions, are rapidly gaining attention in the culinary world.

Fall/Storage Onions *(Also known as cooking onions or dry onions):* Fall/storage onions are available from September through February. Grown specifically for their ability to store well in the winter, they are harvested in the late fall and then cured for winter use. (It is possible to see fall/storage onions in the early spring; they are early harvest onions which have been shipped from a warmer climate, generally southern California or Mexico.) They are typically inexpensive. Generally globular in shape, they have a flavorful, pungent, meaty flesh.

Although not referred to as sweet onions, fall onions have a higher sugar content than their spring kin—often more than a standard ripe apple has. They possess brassy, hearty, full body and rich onion flavors and have firm, concentrated flesh that gives off little aroma until bruised or peeled. But when their sulfuric acid compounds are disturbed, the pungency is released. Heat destroys these compounds, however, and brings out the sugars. Because of their dense flesh, fall/storage onions impart a rich, robust flavor to foods, even after long periods of cooking.

Red Globe: The standard globe-shaped red onion with red skin and flesh. Good for roasting, but its color will turn gray after prolonged cooking.

Sweet Spanish: Large, yellow-skinned, globe-shaped onion with dense, pungent flesh. Full of sugar and great for all types of cooking. Best for onion soup, caramelized onions or to sweeten and flavor sauces and soups.

White Globe: Large, beautiful globe-shaped onion with a spicy and pungent flavor. Highly regarded by Hispanic cooks, it is intensely flavorful and turns pale gold when cooked. It can also be eaten raw, depending upon your tolerance for its spiciness. Use fresh in salads or sandwiches.

Yellow Cooking: Medium-sized, globe-shaped onion with dark brown skin and deep yellow flesh. Considered the best cooking onion, it contains a particularly high concentration of sulfuric compounds, which results in a richer and more pungent flavor than other fall/storage onions. Often sold in bags at the market.

Spring/Summer Onions *(Also known as mild or sweet onions):* Spring/summer onions, available from early April through August, have a short shelf life and are therefore more expensive than fall/storage onions. Typically large, spring/summer onions weigh up to 2 pounds each. They have slightly flattened bulbs and have thinner, crispier skins than fall/storage onions. Spring/summer onions have a spicy bite

when first pulled from the ground. Within days, though, the flavor and heat diminishes. Their flesh is soft, moist and often referred to as sweet. Spring onions actually have a lower sugar content than fall/storage onions; it is their mild, less sulfuric qualities that make us describe them as sweet.

Spring/summer onions, typically grown in warm climates, are marketed under the name of where they are grown. The first spring onions available on the United States market are the Texas Spring Sweets and the California Sweet Imperials, which arrive in early April. By May and June, Georgia Vidalia onions appear. Walla Wallas from Washington arrive last, sometime in July or August. Because these onions are grown in the cooler months of winter, they produce a milder tasting onion.

Spring/summer onions have a juicy, almost fruitlike sweetness that makes them best for eating raw in salads or on sandwiches. They are also recommended for frying onion rings, roasting whole and for quick grilling. They are not good for slow-cooked preparations since they do not produce an intense onion flavor, even over long periods of cooking. Their low sulfur content also causes less tear-jerking.

Granex: Sweet Granex onions are sold under various trade names according to where they are grown, such as Vidalia in Georgia or Maui in Hawaii. These large yellow onions have flattened bulbs and a sweet, mild taste. Best eaten raw in salads or sandwiches or cooked into thick, juicy onion rings.

Grano: Grano onions are also marketed under the name of where they are grown, such as Texas Spring Sweets, New

Mexico Carzalias and California Sweet Imperials. Globe shaped with yellow flesh, they can weigh up to 3 pounds each. The larger they are, the milder they are. Use them raw or quickly cooked for maximum flavor.

Red Spring: Large, flattened bulb with red-and-white flesh that, because of its shape, yields more slices per bulb than many other onions. It has a very mild, extra sweet and succulent flavor. Italian Red is the most commonly sold variety on the market. Also look for Early California and Red Burger, which have similar qualities.

Torpedo: A football-shaped bulb with a mild, sweet flesh. The most commonly available variety, the Red Torpedo, is typically found in farmers' markets. Great for eating raw or grilled, roasted or baked whole.

Walla Walla: Principally grown around Walla Walla, Washington, this round, creamy-fleshed variety is renowned for its sweet and succulent yet crunchy flesh. It can range in size from 3 ounces to 1 1/2 pounds. Delicious raw, grilled, baked whole or as onion rings.

Green Onions/Bunching Onions: Available year-round, but especially good in the early spring and early fall. A green onion is simply a young bulbing onion before its base broadens. The word *scallion* is a commercial name for the green onion. Look for red- and yellow-colored green onions in specialty and farmers' markets.

Bunching onions originate from varieties that do not bulb but instead grow beneath the soil in clusters. Onions labeled at the market as bunching onions are often not genuine bunching onions. They are, instead, immature bulbing onions, or green onions. True bunching onions are only available in select farmers' markets.

Use green and bunching onions in quick sautés and stir-fries or as a fresh, bright finish for pastas, egg dishes or soups. Try dipping whole green onions in batter and deep-frying them as you would onion rings. If you garden, don't cast away onion thinnings. Use them in salads or as a seasoning in place of chives or commercial green onions.

Onion Sprouts: Available year-round in a handful of specialty produce stores. The sprouts of onions (or of leeks or shallots), including the tiny black seeds, are edible and have a piquant, fresh onion flavor. They make a welcome addition to sandwiches and salads and are a flavorful garnish for soups or pastas. Store the sprouts in a lock-top plastic bag or airtight jar in the refrigerator for up to a week.

Pearl Onions: Available year-round. Also known as pickling onions, pearl onions usually range in size from about 5/8 inch to 1 1/2 inches in diameter. Some are globe shaped; others are flatter and look like tiny pumpkins. These onions are best cooked or pickled.

Cipollini: Delicate, white-fleshed, golden-skinned onions with a flattened shape and an exceptional sweet flavor. Slightly larger than most pearl onions, cipollini have a diameter of 1 1/2 to 2 inches and are widely used in Italian cuisine. Use fresh or store for winter. Use for pickling, roasting and boiling and in soups or stews.

Purplette: Small, lavender-fleshed, purple-skinned pearl onion that is good fresh and stores well for months. It retains its lavender coloring when cooked, making it a great addition to kabobs. Add to soups, roasts and stews during the last 15 minutes of cooking.

White Pearl: Small, round, white all-purpose pearl onion with sweet, firm flesh. Great for pickling, roasting or skewering on kabobs. The Barletta is a common variety.

CHIVES *(Allium schoenoprasum):* The most delicate member of the onion family, chives grow in clusters of tiny, deep green, grasslike shoots with hollow cylindrical centers. In season during the spring and summer, they are grown in greenhouses or in warmer climates and shipped year-round. Chives' grassy flavor adds a bright hint of sweet onion without overpowering a dish.

Garlic chives, also known as Chinese chives, have flat, broad leaves and a mild oniony, but distinctly garlicky, flavor. Their white blossoms can be pulled off the stem and used in lieu of the greens as a subtle seasoning or a striking garnish.

GARLIC *(Allium sativum):* Harvested in the springtime, but because of its excellent storage qualities, available year-round. Fresh garlic is dried during the summer and then stored all winter long. By the following spring, you can expect the garlic to be less pungent, somewhat soft and spongy. At that time, substitute with green garlic or freshly dried bulbs imported from warmer climates. Green garlic, the tender young stalks of garlic, can be used like the green onions they resemble. The stalks are harvested before the papery

outer skin has formed on either the cloves or the bulb. They are ideal used raw or cooked to impart foods with a mild garlic and onion flavor.

California Early: Large, flat, round bulbs with lots of plump cloves and pinkish beige papery skin. This is the first commercial garlic to hit the market in the spring and summer, and it is sweeter and milder than California Late. It is not, however, a good storage garlic. Great all-purpose garlic for cooking.

California Late: Its long storage qualities make this the most commonly found garlic in the grocery store. It forms large, white-sheathed, artichoke-shaped bulbs and is distinguished from other varieties by the green, papery skin surrounding the bulb. It has irregularly shaped cloves and a good spicy bite that makes it an excellent all-purpose garlic.

Elephant Garlic: A relative of the leek rather than a true garlic, elephant garlic has a shape and flavor that give it its garlic allegiance. The bulb and cloves are much larger than those of regular garlic, and the flavor is mild, which means it is not a good substitute for regular garlic in cooking. It is acceptable for roasting because the large cloves make peeling easy.

Rocambole: Carried in specialty grocery stores, Rocambole has light purplish skin and plump, cream-colored cloves. It is the garlic of choice in European kitchens because of its rich, intense flavor. Its hot and spicy nature calls for care when using it raw.

LEEKS *(Allium porrum):* Available year-round in most climates. Looking like giant green onions, leeks have a flavor and fragrance milder than those of onions or garlic. Often referred to as the poor man's asparagus, leeks traditionally have been used as a seasoning in soups, sauces and vegetable dishes. Today, cooks are commonly looking upon the leek as a vegetable in its own right.

Blue Solaise: A beautiful heirloom leek that takes on a violet hue when grown in colder climates. This variety is great for oven roasting, stewing and grilling and for slicing thinly onto salads or pastas.

Large American Flag (Broad London): The most common of the leek variety, grown both for commercial use and in home gardens. A hardy plant that can withstand colder growing conditions, it produces thick stems, with the blanched portion growing from 1 to 2 inches in diameter. Its distinctive flavor makes it good for oven roasting and for adding to soups, sautés, stews and sauces.

SHALLOTS *(Allium cepa):* Available year-round in most climates. Many cooks describe the flavor of the shallot as a cross between an onion and garlic. Shallots are available with red, gray and yellow-brown skins, with the red shallot being the mildest of the three.

The shallot has a much milder and softer taste than the bulbing onion. When harvested at a tender age, the whole plant can be eaten as one would a young green onion or leek, but shallots are more commonly used when they have formed a bulb about 2 inches in length.

Growing Your Own Onions:

Bulbing Onions: Once you have determined what kind of onion seeds or sets are suitable for where you live, growing onions is easy. Should you run into problems and bulbing fails to occur, don't throw the plants away. The shoots are delicious used as you might use green onions or leeks.

Onions bulb in relation to the amount of light they receive during their growing season, and the amount of light is determined by where you live. Consult seed catalogues to distinguish whether the seeds, sets, or plants are short-day or long-day varieties. Short-day varieties are best planted in southern regions, between 24 degrees and 28 degrees latitude, which, in the United States, falls in southern Texas and in parts of Florida and Georgia. Long-day varieties should be grown in regions that fall north of 36 degrees latitude. If you live in the north, sow seeds or plant sets as soon as the soil can be worked for harvesting fall onions. If you live in the south, plant in the fall or winter months for a spring harvest.

Soil should be well fertilized, full of humus, have good drainage and be kept well weeded at all times. Water every other day until the greens are about 2 inches tall, and then keep the soil moist, watering once a week, or more if you live in a very hot climate. Harvest onions throughout their growing season; use thinnings and young onions raw for cooking.

Onion bulbs are ready to harvest when the greens wilt and begin to turn brown and a thin, papery skin begins to form. Dig up the bulbs and spread them out to cure in a place where air can circulate around them, out of direct sunlight and away from the threat of rain. Let the onions cure for a week or two until the greens turn brown.

Onion Sprouts: To grow your own sprouts, place 2 table-spoons of onion seeds in a wide-mouthed jar and cover the top with gauze or fine-mesh netting. Secure the gauze to the lip of the jar with a rubber band. Place the jar on its side on a well-lit windowsill. Rinse the onion seeds (through the gauze) with water daily, draining off excess moisture, for about 10 days, or until the sprouts are about 1 inch long.

Chives: Both common chives and garlic chives are among the easiest herbs to grow. Plant chives from seed, or ask to dig up a cluster from your neighbor's herb garden. They do not need much water, but do grow best in rich soil. Chives prosper in a garden plot as well as in pots on a sunny windowsill. To harvest, use scissors and snip off as much as you need. The trimming seems to make them grow better and stronger, so use chives as often as possible in place of green onions.

Garlic: Plant garlic in early spring in dark, humus-rich soil in a very sunny spot as soon as the ground is workable. Slip single cloves, broad end down, into the soil 2 inches deep and about 3 inches apart. Keep moist until the greens begin to wilt; the bulbs are then ready to harvest. Pull up and cure in the sun for at least 2 weeks. Garlic can be harvested and eaten throughout its growing season, from mild green sprouts through mature, hot, spicy bulbs.

Leeks: Leeks are easy to grow. They are relatively pest-free and will do well in nearly any climate. Seeds should be sown in February, either indoors in the north or outdoors in the south. They like nitrogen-rich soil, plenty of water, and must be planted 6 to 8 inches deep and 3 to 6 inches apart.

Blanching leeks (whitening the leaves) is achieved by mound-ing dirt around the stem as it emerges from the topsoil. To keep leeks as clean as possible, slip a paper or plastic tube 2 inches in diameter over each plant and mound dirt around the base. As the plant grows, move the tube upward and remound the dirt to cover the base and the blanched leaves. Harvest baby leeks whenever you like. For mature leeks, dig up the plants when they are more than 1 inch in diameter.

Shallots: In early spring, or as soon as the ground softens, plant individual shallot cloves, broad end down, in rich soil about 1 inch deep and 6 inches apart. Water throughout the growing season. Harvest throughout the season as well, using thinnings as you would chives or green garlic. The bulbs are ready to harvest when the greens are about 8 inches high and the plant is completely dried out. Cure in the sun for 2 weeks until the greens turn brown.

Recommended Seed Sources

Filaree Farm
Route 2, P.O. Box 162
Okanogan, Washington 98840
Large selection of garlic

Lockhart Seeds, Inc.
P.O. Box 1361
3 North Wilson Way
Stockton, California 95205
Large selection of onions

Park Seed Company
Cokesbury Road
Greenwood, South Carolina
29647
Large selection of onions and garlic

Shepherd's Garden Seeds
30 Irene Street
Torrington, Connecticut 06790
Specialty onions, garlic and shallots

Stokes Seeds, Inc.
P.O. Box 548
Buffalo, New York 14240
Large selection of onions

OPENERS

When I was a child, and guests were about to arrive at our home, my mother would often have a pan of onions frying on the stove. She convinced me that these aromas were warm and inviting. I continue to be inspired by her example and create oniony first courses to fill my house with the fragrance of hospitality.

Many restaurants offer onion soup as a starter, evidence that there must be some truth to this theory. This dish can be made any time of the year, but it is best in the fall and winter, when pungent cooking onions are in the market.

Most of the time, onions, garlic or leeks are cooked until soft and sweet as the first step in the preparation of a memorable soup or stew. Yet, fresh green onions, tender chive blades or mild leeks can also act as a lively seasoning or a stunning finish for all kinds of dishes.

Friends regularly remark on how often they find a platter of roasted or grilled onions, leeks and garlic sitting on my dining room table to welcome them. Depending upon the season, the grilled vegetables will be teamed with warm figs, wild mushrooms, roasted eggplant and peppers or thick slices of juicy red tomatoes. Other times, we might start our evening by getting giddy with martinis garnished with vermouth-laced pearl onions, munching on appetizers and skipping the main course altogether.

Onion Soup with Crispy Shallots and Gruyère Toasts

This is a light version of the classic onion soup. Its success lies in the pungency of the onions. I recommend fall/storage onions because of the full-bodied flavors they impart. For a simpler preparation, omit the crispy shallot garnish.

Soup:
5 tablespoons unsalted butter
1 1/2 pounds yellow onions thinly sliced
1/2 pound shallots, thinly sliced
3 tablespoons unbleached white flour
6 cups beef stock or Leek, Onion and Mushroom
    Stock (recipe p.65), or other vegetable stock
1/2 cup ruby port
1/4 cup Cognac, or to taste
4 bay leaves
6 to 8 sprigs fresh thyme
10 whole black peppercorns, lightly crushed
1 carrot, left whole
Salt, to taste

Toasts:
8 slices sweet French bread, each 1/2 inch thick
1/2 pound Gruyère or other good-quality
    Swiss-type cheese, grated or thinly sliced

Crispy Shallot Garnish:
Vegetable oil, for deep-frying
1 cup unbleached white flour
1/4 cup cornstarch
Salt, paprika and freshly ground black pepper, to taste
1/2 pound shallots, thinly sliced

Chopped fresh parsley, for garnish (optional)

To make the soup, melt the butter in a large, heavy-bottomed pot over medium heat. Add the onions and shallots and sauté for approximately 20 minutes, or until soft and caramelized. Sprinkle the flour over the onions and shallots, stir and cook for a few minutes longer.

Pour in the stock, port and Cognac and add the bay leaves, thyme, peppercorns and carrot. Bring to a boil, reduce the heat to low and simmer, uncovered, for approximately 45 minutes, or until slightly thickened and caramel in color. Remove the carrot, bay leaves and thyme sprigs and discard. Season with salt.

To make the toasts, preheat the broiler or oven to 400 degrees F. Arrange the bread slices on a baking sheet and top with cheese. Toast under the broiler or in the oven until the cheese is melted and lightly browned. Set aside.

To make the shallot garnish, in a deep, heavy-bottomed skillet pour in the oil to a depth of 1 1/2 inches and heat until it just begins to smoke. In a medium-sized bowl, stir together the flour and cornstarch and the salt, paprika and black pepper to taste. When the oil is hot, coat the shallot slices evenly with the flour mixture, shaking off any excess. Working in batches and keeping the shallots from sticking together, drop the shallots in the hot oil and fry for 4 or 5 minutes, or until crisp and golden brown. Using a slotted spoon, remove to paper towels to drain. Taste and season with salt.

Place a Gruyère toast in the bottom of each bowl. Ladle some of the onion soup on top. Place a second toast on top and spoon in more hot soup. Garnish with crispy shallots and chopped parsley. *Serves 4*

*Left to right: Purple Potato, Garlic and Leek Soup (recipe p. 26) and
Onion Soup with Crispy Shallots and Gruyère Toasts*

Purple Potato, Garlic and Leek Soup

This soup was created by my son Joshua's college friends Eric Toshalis and Sheri Kalbaugh, who share my sense of intrigue with new and unusual foods. It combines the lavender bulbs and tender green tops of very young leeks with purple Peruvian potatoes and green zucchini to create a beautiful modern rendition of old-fashioned potato-leek soup. If you can't find purple leeks or potatoes, this robust soup is equally delicious made with conventional white leeks and potatoes. Green onions or green garlic can be substituted for the leeks. This goes nicely with slices of warm whole-wheat bread.

2 bunches very young, tender purple leeks such as
    Blue Solaise (approximately 12)
3 tablespoons unsalted butter
5 cloves garlic
4 cups Leek, Onion and Mushroom Stock
    (recipe p.65) or any other vegetable or
    chicken stock

1 1/2 pounds purple potatoes, peeled and cut into
    1 1/2-inch cubes
3 medium-sized zucchini (approximately 1 pound),
    cut into 1/2-inch cubes
3 tablespoons finely chopped fresh parsley
1/2 to 3/4 cup heavy cream
Salt and coarsely ground black pepper, to taste

Trim the leeks and rinse carefully. Thinly slice the white portion and any tender green portions. Set the green portions aside.

Melt the butter in a large saucepan over low heat. Add the sliced white leek portions and garlic and sauté for 5 to 8 minutes, or until softened. Add the stock and bring to a boil. Add the potatoes, reduce the heat and simmer, uncovered, for approximately 10 to 15 minutes, or until the potatoes are soft when pierced.

Remove from the heat. Working in batches, purée the soup in a food processor or blender. Return the purée to the saucepan. Add the zucchini and the reserved sliced leek greens to the saucepan and bring to a simmer. Cook, uncovered, for 5 minutes.

Add the parsley and stir in enough cream to thin the soup to the desired consistency. Heat to serving temperature and season with salt and pepper. Ladle into bowls and serve immediately. *Serves 4 to 6*

Beet, Potato and Onion Latkes with Lox Schmere

When I was a child, we ate latkes not only at our Chanukah celebration, but also as a side dish with roasted meats for dinner or with smoked fish and sour cream for brunch. My mother always added a heavy measure of onions, making my family's version of latkes moist and aromatic. The Yiddish word "schmere" means "spread," and this particular schmere complements the combination of beets and potatoes perfectly.

Latkes:

1 medium-sized russet potato
2 medium-sized red beets
2 medium-sized yellow onions
3 eggs, lightly beaten
1 teaspoon salt
1/4 teaspoon freshly ground black pepper
5 tablespoons bleached white flour, or more if needed
1 teaspoon baking powder
1 cup vegetable oil

Lox Schmere:

4 ounces cream cheese, at room temperature
4 ounces lox, finely chopped
1 tablespoon chopped fresh dill
1 tablespoon chopped fresh garlic chives
1 tablespoon drained capers
1/4 teaspoon white pepper
Few dashes of Worcestershire sauce

1 tablespoon chopped fresh garlic chives, for garnish

To make the latkes, peel and then grate the potatoes, beets and onions on the coarse side of a hand grater. Using your hands, gather together the grated vegetables and squeeze them to press out as much liquid as possible so that they will not be heavy. (Alternatively, wrap them in a piece of cheesecloth or a kitchen towel and press out the liquid.)

In a medium-sized bowl, combine all the grated ingredients and the eggs and stir to mix. In a smaller bowl, stir together the salt, pepper, 5 tablespoons flour and the baking powder. Add the flour mixture to the egg mixture and mix thoroughly.

In a large, heavy-bottomed skillet, heat the oil until it just begins to smoke. Being careful not to crowd the pan, drop the latke batter by tablespoonfuls into the hot oil and flatten slightly with the back of a spoon or a spatula. Each pancake should be about 1 1/2 to 2 inches in diameter. If you see that the batter is not holding together, add another tablespoon of flour to the remaining batter. Turn down the heat as necessary to prevent burning and cook for approximately 2 minutes, or until well browned on the first side. Using a spatula, flip the cakes and fry for approximately 2 minutes longer, or until well browned on the second side. Transfer to paper towels to drain. You should have 20 latkes in all.

To make the schmere, in a bowl, stir together the cream cheese, lox, dill, garlic chives, capers, white pepper and Worcestershire sauce until well blended.

Spoon some of the schmere on the tops of half of the pancakes. Top with the remaining pancakes and press down lightly to flatten. Arrange on individual plates and garnish with the chives. Serve warm or at room temperature. *Makes 10 small sandwiches; serves 5*

Shallot Garlic Flan with Roasted Garlic Cloves

*The first time I ate at the famed Fog City Diner in San Francisco, I asked the waiter
what he thought was the best dish coming out of the kitchen. Without hesitation, he leaned over
and whispered, "Have you had the garlic flan?" I ordered it, and from the first bite I knew
I had found garlic nirvana. In this version, the shallots give the flan a denser texture.*

Roasted Garlic:
18 or more cloves garlic, peeled but left whole
Light olive oil
2 sprigs fresh parsley or rosemary

Flan:
4 large shallots, coarsely chopped
*2 garlic bulbs, cloves separated, peeled and
    coarsely chopped*

2 cups heavy cream
6 sprigs fresh thyme
Pinch of freshly grated nutmeg
1/2 teaspoon salt
1/4 teaspoon white pepper
4 egg yolks
2 tablespoons chopped fresh chives
Boiling water, as needed

To roast the garlic, preheat the oven to 350 degrees F. Coat the garlic cloves lightly with olive oil and place on a sheet of aluminum foil along with the herb sprigs. Wrap securely and roast for approximately 30 minutes, or until the cloves are soft when pierced with a knife. Set aside the cloves to use as a garnish. Reduce the oven temperature to 275 degrees F.

While the garlic is roasting, begin to make the flan. In a medium-sized saucepan over medium heat, combine the shallots, garlic, cream, thyme, nutmeg, salt and pepper. Bring to a gentle simmer and cook uncovered, stirring occasionally, until the mixture is reduced by approximately 1/3, or until it is thick enough to coat the back of a wooden spoon.

Remove from the heat and discard the thyme sprigs. Strain the mixture through a fine-mesh sieve into a bowl, pressing against the sieve with the back of a spoon to extract as much of the liquid as possible.

In another bowl, whisk the egg yolks until well blended; then whisk the yolks into the strained mixture until thoroughly incorporated.

Lightly butter six 1/2-cup ovenproof custard cups. Sprinkle an equal amount of the chives into the bottom of each cup. Pour the egg mixture into the cups, dividing it evenly among them. Place the filled cups in a baking pan or dish with 2-inch sides. Cover the cups with aluminum foil. Then pour boiling water into the pan or dish to reach within 1/2 inch of the rim of the cups.

Bake for approximately 1 hour, or until the flans are firm. To test, insert the tip of a knife into the center of a flan; it should come out clean.

Serve the flans warm. Garnish each flan with some of the roasted garlic cloves. *Serves 6*

Roasted Whole Garlic Bulbs and Wild Mushrooms on Arugula

Mushrooms and garlic go hand in hand. When you are roasting the garlic for this recipe, throw in a few extra bulbs. They keep for days and the resulting heady garlic purée is great spread on bread. Remember, garlic is good for you. You can never eat too much of it.

Roasted Garlic:
4 firm whole garlic bulbs
Olive oil
Salt and freshly ground black pepper, to taste
2 tablespoons chopped fresh marjoram (optional)

Roasted Mushrooms:
4 large fresh portobello, chanterelle or shiitake mushrooms
1/2 cup extra virgin olive oil
4 to 5 tablespoons red wine vinegar
4 cloves garlic, chopped

1 tablespoon finely chopped fresh oregano
1 tablespoon finely chopped fresh rosemary
2 tablespoons finely chopped red onion
1 tablespoon brown sugar
Salt and freshly ground black pepper, to taste

1/2 pound arugula, tough stems discarded
1/2 red bell pepper, seeded, deribbed and finely chopped
4 whole garlic chive blossoms (optional)
1 loaf crusty white bread

To roast the garlic, preheat the oven to 375 degrees F. Remove any loose papery skins from the garlic, but do not peel or separate. Coat the garlic bulbs with olive oil and then sprinkle with salt, pepper and the marjoram, if using. Seal them individually or together in aluminum foil.

Roast for 30 to 60 minutes, depending on size; the cloves should be soft when pierced with a sharp knife. Remove from the oven, unwrap and let cool. Then, using a sharp knife or a serrated bread knife, cut off the top of each bulb, being sure to expose the top of the cloves.

While the garlic is roasting, begin preparing the mushrooms. Trim off any tough stems and then, using a soft, dry cloth or a mushroom brush, whisk off any dirt from the mushrooms. Using a sharp knife, score each mushroom cap in a shallow crisscross pattern to enable the basting mixture to penetrate the flesh.

In a medium-sized bowl, stir together the olive oil, vinegar, chopped garlic, oregano, rosemary, onion, brown sugar, salt and pepper. Let stand for approximately 15 minutes.

When the garlic is cooked, increase the oven temperature to 500 degrees F. Dip the mushrooms in the oil mixture, coating completely, and place them on a baking sheet. Roast for 5 to 7 minutes, or until they begin to soften, brown and release their moisture.

Divide the arugula among 4 dinner plates. Place 1 whole garlic bulb and 1 hot roasted mushroom on each plate. Drizzle any pan juices or remaining basting mixture evenly over the arugula. Garnish the plates with a scattering of chopped bell pepper. Remove the petals from the garlic chive blossoms, if using, and scatter on top. Break the bread into rough pieces and serve alongside. *Serves 4*

Warm Spinach Salad with Onion and Caper Vinaigrette

The secret to this salad is the slow cooking of the onion in the vinaigrette. The vinaigrette can be used on almost any salad, but in combination with tender young spinach leaves, feta, mushrooms and leeks, it is a meal in itself.

2/3 cup extra virgin olive oil
1 large red onion, thinly sliced
2 tablespoons capers, including a little of the brine
2 cloves garlic, chopped
1/4 cup balsamic vinegar
Salt and freshly ground pepper, to taste
2 medium-sized leeks, washed and thinly sliced

1/4 pound fresh shiitake or domestic mushrooms,
   thinly sliced
1 teaspoon chopped fresh thyme
2 bunches spinach (medium-sized leaves), stems
   removed, and carefully rinsed and dried
6 ounces feta cheese, crumbled

In a small sauté pan over low heat, warm the olive oil. Add the onion and sauté for approximately 5 minutes, or until softened. Add the capers and brine, garlic and balsamic vinegar and stir well. Season with salt and pepper and remove from the heat.

Transfer 2 tablespoons of the warm olive oil mixture to another medium-sized sauté pan and place over low heat. Add the leeks and sauté for approximately 3 minutes, or until limp. Add the mushrooms and thyme and sauté for approximately 3 to 4 minutes, or until softened. Remove from the heat.

Combine the spinach and feta in a large bowl or on a platter and toss to mix. Return the pan holding the olive oil mixture to the stove and heat until very hot. When it is hot, pour it over the spinach and feta and toss thoroughly. Scatter the sautéed leeks and mushrooms over the top. Transfer to individual plates and serve immediately. *Serves 4*

*Clockwise from the back: Asian Pear and Sweet Onion Salad with Stilton (recipe p. 38),
a platter of Tomato, Sardine and Sweet Onion Salad (recipe p. 34), Whole Onions Stuffed with Pine Nuts
and Basil (recipe p. 37), and Cucumber, Sweet Onion and Spring Ginger Salad (recipe p. 34), and
New Potatoes Wrapped in Prosciutto with Sweet Pepper Soubise*

New Potatoes Wrapped in Prosciutto with Sweet Pepper Soubise

*Soubise is a classic French sauce made by cooking onions in butter until they are soft and sweet,
and then puréeing them with cream or stock. I have taken it a step further by incorporating sweet peppers
into the purée. Any leftover sauce can be stored in the refrigerator for up to a week. It marries well with grilled fish,
is delicious tossed with pasta or can be used as a garnish for scrambled eggs.*

18 small new potatoes (approximately 1 1/2 inches
    in diameter), unpeeled

Soubise:

1 1/2 tablespoons unsalted butter or olive oil
3/4 pound yellow onions (preferably spring/summer
    or early fall/storage), quartered

1 large or 2 medium-sized sweet red bell peppers,
    quartered, seeded and deribbed
Salt and white pepper, to taste
1 tablespoon brown sugar, or to taste

18 small fresh basil leaves, plus fresh basil leaves
    for garnish
9 thin slices prosciutto di Parma, cut in half lengthwise

Pour water into a steamer pan and bring to a boil. Top with the steamer rack and arrange the potatoes on the rack. Cover and steam for approximately 10 minutes, or until the potatoes are tender when pierced with a knife. Remove the potatoes from the steamer, let cool and refrigerate until well chilled.

To make the *soubise*, preheat the oven to 325 degrees F. If using butter, place it in a baking dish large enough to accommodate the vegetables and place the dish in the oven until the butter melts. If using olive oil, simply pour it into the dish. Place the onions and peppers in the dish, cover and bake for approximately 45 minutes, or until both the onions and peppers are very soft when pierced. Stir the vegetables occasionally while they are baking.

Remove the vegetables from the pan and let them cool until they can be handled. If possible, slip off the skins from the peppers. In a food processor or blender, combine the cooked onions, peppers, and all the pan juices and purée until smooth. Thin with a few tablespoons of water if the sauce seems too thick. Season with salt and pepper. If the sauce tastes a little bitter, add the brown sugar. Cover and refrigerate if not using immediately. You will have about 2 cups.

To assemble, spread a medium-sized platter with a thick coating of the *soubise*. Place a basil leaf on top of each potato, and wrap a piece of prosciutto around the potato. Arrange the wrapped potatoes on the platter and garnish with extra basil leaves. *Serves 6 to 8*

Tomato, Sardine and Sweet Onion Salad

During my search for ways to encourage the eating of raw onions, I was offered this idea by a friend, who used to devour just such a salad in an Italian trattoria on the shores of the Mediterranean.

1 large red, yellow or white onion (preferably
    spring/summer), thickly sliced
2 celery stalks, thinly sliced
10 dry-packed sun-dried tomatoes, soaked in
    hot water to cover for 5 minutes, drained and
    finely chopped
3 tablespoons drained capers
1/2 cup extra virgin olive oil
1/4 cup red wine vinegar
2 tablespoons chopped fresh oregano
Salt and freshly ground pepper, to taste
2 or 3 medium-sized vine-ripened red or
    yellow tomatoes, thickly sliced
8 to 12 high-quality, plump fresh-cured or
    canned sardines, drained
12 salt-cured Italian black olives

In a medium-sized bowl, combine the onion, celery, sun-dried tomatoes, capers, oil, vinegar and oregano. Let stand at room temperature for 30 minutes. Season with salt and pepper.

Place 2 or 3 fresh tomato slices on each of 4 salad plates. Top generously with the marinated onions. Finish each dish with 2 or 3 whole sardines and a scattering of olives and serve. *Serves 4*

Cucumber, Sweet Onion and Spring Ginger Salad

This refreshing salad is frequently consumed by my youngest son, Jonah, straight out of the bowl, before it ever gets a chance to be served at the table.

2 medium-sized cucumbers
1 small red onion (preferably spring/summer),
    sliced paper-thin
1/4 cup finely chopped young spring ginger
3 tablespoons cider vinegar
2 tablespoons granulated sugar or honey
Salt and freshly ground black pepper, to taste
2 tablespoons sour cream (optional)

Peel the cucumbers lengthwise, leaving some of the skin intact to form an overall striped pattern. Slice the cucumbers crosswise into thin rounds.

In a medium-sized bowl, combine the cucumbers, onion, ginger, vinegar and sugar or honey. Toss and let stand for 15 minutes. Season with salt and pepper. Add the sour cream if you want a slightly creamy salad. Cover and refrigerate to chill well before serving. *Serves 4*

Front to back: Tomato, Sardine and Sweet Onion Salad, Whole Onions Stuffed with Pine Nuts and Basil (recipe p. 37) and Cucumber, Sweet Onion and Spring Ginger Salad

Whole Onions Stuffed with Pine Nuts and Basil

Stuffed onions were popular on European dining tables in the late 1800s.
This rendition is a spin-off of a recipe my grandmother used for stuffing artichokes.
Seek out the Red Torpedo variety for a particularly spectacular presentation.

3 tablespoons pine nuts
6 medium-sized red, yellow or white onions,
*   unpeeled*
1 1/2 cups fresh bread crumbs
4 cloves garlic, minced
1/2 cup finely chopped fresh basil

4 heaping tablespoons grated Asiago cheese
3 tablespoons olive oil
2 eggs, lightly beaten
Salt and freshly ground black pepper, to taste
1/2 cup water or chicken stock
3 to 4 tablespoons balsamic vinegar

Preheat the oven to 350 degrees F. Spread the pine nuts in a small pan and place in the oven for 5 to 10 minutes, or until lightly browned. Set the nuts aside. Leave the oven set at 350 degrees F.

Meanwhile, peel off the onion skins. Cut off the stem end from each onion, but leave the root end intact. Bring a large saucepan three-fourths full of water to a boil. Add the onions and boil for approximately 15 minutes, or until slightly softened. Drain and immerse in cold water to cool.

When the onions are cool, drain well. Cut a slice about 3/4 inch thick off the top of each onion. Scoop out as much of the onion flesh as you can, leaving as thin a shell as possible, but one that will maintain its shape during baking. Set the shells aside. Finely chop the removed onion pulp.

To make the stuffing, in a medium-sized bowl, combine the bread crumbs, garlic, basil, Asiago cheese, toasted pine nuts and chopped onion. Stir to mix well. In a small bowl, stir together the olive oil and eggs until blended. Pour the oil mixture into the bread crumb mixture, stirring until fully incorporated. Add a little water as needed to moisten. Season with salt and pepper.

Using a sharp knife, cut off the root end of each onion. Fill each onion cavity with an equal amount of the stuffing.

Place the stuffed onions, root end down, in a medium-sized roasting pan. Pour the water or stock and the balsamic vinegar into the pan. Cover loosely with aluminum foil and bake for approximately 30 minutes. Remove the foil, raise the heat to 375 degrees F. and roast for another 15 minutes, or until the onions are tender when pierced and the stuffing is browned. Serve warm or at room temperature. *Serves 6*

Asian Pear and Sweet Onion Salad with Stilton

*I first made this salad for a farmers' market celebration. The onions had just been
picked that morning. They were crunchy and spicy and complemented the musty pears and
tangy cheese. The feast was set out on the tailgate of a dusty old truck, and we drank Champagne
to toast the harvest and the organic farmers who had made our celebration possible.*

1/2 cup walnut halves
2 Asian pears, quartered, cored and thinly sliced
1 medium-sized red, white or yellow onion
    (preferably spring/summer), thinly sliced
1 tablespoon chopped fresh thyme

4 ounces Stilton or other good-quality blue cheese
Juice of 1 very sweet orange
2 tablespoons extra virgin olive oil
1 tablespoon chopped fresh chives
Handful of berries or orange slices, for garnish

Preheat the oven to 350 degrees F. Spread the walnuts in a small pan and place in the oven for 5 to 10 minutes, or until lightly toasted.

In a large bowl, toss together the pears, onion, thyme and toasted walnuts. Crumble the Stilton cheese over the top and then drizzle with the orange juice and olive oil. Garnish with the chives and the berries or orange slices, if using. Serve immediately. *Serves 6*

"Martini Magic" Pearl Onions, Olives and Lemon Rind in Vermouth

When the day has gotten the best of me, I head straight for a very dry gin martini crowned with a homemade cocktail onion. Presoaking the olives, onions and lemon rind in vermouth eliminates the need to add any vermouth to your drink. All you have to do is ice the gin, kick off your shoes and remember how good life can be after all.

4 cups cold water
1/2 basket small red or white pearl onions
    (15 to 25 onions) or small shallots
Ice water, to cover
1 firm lemon

1 jar (10 ounces) pimiento-stuffed green olives,
    drained
Dry vermouth, to cover
1 fresh hot red chili pepper such as cayenne or
    jalapeño (optional)

In a medium-sized saucepan over high heat, bring the cold water to a boil. Meanwhile, cut off the root ends of the onions. Have ready a large bowl of ice water.

Drop the trimmed onions into the boiling water for approximately 5 minutes. You want the onions to be cooked but still have some crunch. Drain and transfer to the ice water. When cool, drain and peel.

Using a sharp knife, remove the rind from the lemon, being careful not to include any of the bitter white membrane. Slice it into narrow uniform strips about 2 inches long. Set aside.

Sterilize a quart jar with a tight-fitting lid. Then layer the onions, olives and lemon rind in the jar. Add vermouth to cover completely and slip in the chili pepper if you want to spice up your martinis. Cover and refrigerate overnight before using. The mixture will keep for weeks in the refrigerator.

When making a martini, use a vermouth-soaked olive, onion or lemon rind strip in place of a splash of vermouth. *Makes 1 quart*

Roasted Onions and Figs with Gorgonzola Croutons

I created this dish when I came upon figs and freshly pulled Red Torpedo onions side by side on a table at my local farmers' market. The combination of red onions, doused with a bit of balsamic vinegar, succulent ripe figs and pungent Gorgonzola cheese is a taste sensation you won't forget. This is one recipe in which cooking red onions produces an eye-appealing dish. Leeks can also be prepared this same way.

6 medium-sized red onions (preferably
    spring/summer), with greens intact
3 tablespoons extra virgin olive oil
2 tablespoons chopped garlic
1 teaspoon salt, or to taste
1/2 teaspoon freshly ground black pepper, or to taste
1/2 cup chopped fresh mint
12 firm yet ripe fresh figs or dried figs
1/4 cup balsamic vinegar

Croutons:
5 to 6 ounces Gorgonzola cheese,
    at room temperature
Generous dash of Tabasco sauce
Generous dash of Worcestershire sauce
Approximately 3 tablespoons milk or heavy cream
18 thin slices baguette
1/4 cup olive oil, scented with 2 crushed cloves
    of garlic

Preheat the oven to 350 degrees F.

Rinse the onions well and trim off the greens to within 3 to 5 inches above the bulbs, but do not peel. Cut the onions in half from stem to root end. In a medium-sized bowl, stir together the olive oil, garlic, salt, pepper and mint. Using your hands, thoroughly coat the onions with the mixture and place them in a shallow baking dish. Bake for 30 minutes.

Add the figs to the baking dish and baste with the dish juices. Continue roasting the onions and figs for another 15 minutes, or until the onions are soft when pierced with a knife. Remove from the oven and drizzle generously with the balsamic vinegar. Set aside to cool to room temperature.

While the onions and figs are cooking, begin to make the croutons. In a medium-sized bowl, stir together the Gorgonzola and the Tabasco and Worcestershire sauces until smooth. Thin with enough milk or cream to make the mixture spreadable. Set aside at room temperature.

Raise the oven temperature to 400 degrees F. Brush the baguette slices on both sides with the garlic-scented olive oil and arrange on a baking sheet. Bake for approximately 10 minutes, or until browned.

Spread a generous spoonful of the Gorgonzola mixture on top of each crouton. Arrange the onions and figs on a platter and surround with croutons. Serve immediately.
Serves 6

ACCOMPANIMENTS

Before turning the page and getting out your pots and pans, don't forget the considerable appeal of uncooked onions on their own or as a spirited condiment. Small plates of spicy onion sprouts, chopped piquant garlic chives or thin slices of crisp, mild shallots can bring new life to bowls of steaming soup or an otherwise plain cheese pizza.

Next, move to a spicy salad of purple cabbage with papaya, pomegranates and chives for a lovely holiday dish. The Sweet and Spicy Red Onion Marmalade will broaden the flavors of a platter of smoked chicken or do justice to warm toast served next to scrambled eggs and bacon.

Onion-scented oils and vinegars give an extra boost to everything from salad dressings and sauces to sautés. In a similar vein, Pickled Garlic, Turnips and Cucumbers, English in style, pairs perfectly with a plate of salty cheeses, smoky sandwich meats or hard-cooked eggs.

Believe me when I say that the irresistible scent of onions wafting from the kitchen is a sublime way to wake someone in the morning. Pull out the bed tray and load it up with cups of freshly brewed Italian-roast coffee and a plate of fragrant Spicy Green Onion Corn Muffins or Onion Confit Overnight Breakfast Rolls or the Winter Squash and Onion Cheddar Torta. You will see what I mean.

Garlic Bulbils in Olive Oil, Lemon and Oregano

*Each spring, I search the farmer's market for garlic bulbils, which are garlic blossoms before
they burst open and display their delicate, white, garlic-scented petals. The bulbil and most of its tender
green stem are edible. They are tender and fragrant and taste like a garlicky baby asparagus.*

12 to 16 garlic bulbils
1 tablespoon extra virgin olive oil
Juice of 1/2 lemon
*1 tablespoon chopped fresh herbs such as oregano, basil,
   tarragon, marjoram or Italian parsley, or to taste*

2 cloves garlic, chopped
Salt and freshly ground pepper, to taste
1/4 cup olive oil
Shaved Parmesan cheese (optional)

Leaving about 3 inches of stem below the bulbils intact, slice the remaining bulbil stems into 2-inch pieces.

Over a medium-sized pot of boiling water, steam the garlic bulbils and stems for about 3 to 5 minutes. Test a stem piece to be sure that it is tender. Remove from the steamer and place in a medium-sized bowl. Add 1 tablespoon olive oil, the lemon juice, herbs and garlic cloves and toss. Season with salt and pepper. Toss with the olive oil and shaved Parmesan, if using, and serve immediately.

Serves 4

Left to right: Sweet and Spicy Red Onion Marmalade (recipe p. 50), Olive Oil Infused with Red Onion and Garlic, Pickled Garlic, Turnips and Cucumbers (recipe p. 50) and Vinegar Scented with Garlic and Herbs

Vinegar Scented with Garlic and Herbs

Scented vinegars are miraculous additions to salad dressings, plus their herbaceous flavors mean that you can reduce the amount of oil used. These vinegars should be as beautiful to look at as they are to taste. When assembling the herbs and flowers, let your romantic nature take hold. Remember, your flowers must be free of any harmful sprays or other chemicals.

2 tablespoons granulated sugar
4 or 5 whole black peppercorns
1/2 teaspoon whole mustard seeds
3 or 4 cloves garlic
1 to 3 sprigs fresh tarragon, dill or basil (amount depends upon size of herbs)
5 to 7 edible blossoms, such as roses, nasturtiums, borage, or herb blossoms such as sage, thyme or garlic (optional)
4 cups rice wine vinegar

Place the sugar, peppercorns, mustard seeds, garlic, herbs and the blossoms, if using, in a sterilized bottle. Pour in the vinegar and shake vigorously. Cover or cork airtight. After 15 minutes, shake vigorously again to ensure that all the sugar has dissolved. Store for at least 1 week in a cool place before using.

Strain before using, if desired. The vinegar will keep in the refrigerator for up to 3 months. *Makes 1 quart*

Olive Oil Infused with Red Onion and Garlic

This infused oil is convenient because you don't have to chop garlic or onion each time you want to impart their flavors to a dish. I use this oil for everything from salads to sautés.
Do not discard the simmered onion and garlic. Season them further with fresh herbs and use as a pasta sauce, or purée them, then add vinegar and spices, and serve as a thick, naturally creamy salad dressing.

4 cups extra virgin olive oil
1 medium-sized red onion (fall/storage), thinly sliced
6 to 8 cloves garlic, cut in half
1 large sprig fresh rosemary (optional)
1 chipotle pepper (optional)

Combine the olive oil, red onion and garlic in a heavy-bottomed saucepan. Place over low heat, bring to a simmer and cook for approximately 15 minutes. Remove from the heat and let cool to room temperature.

In a fine-mesh sieve (or a sieve lined with cheesecloth), strain the olive oil into a clean container, then transfer to a sterilized bottle. At this time, you can season the oil further by slipping a rosemary sprig or, for a smoky oil, a chipotle pepper into the bottle. Cover and refrigerate for up to 2 weeks. *Makes 4 cups*

Pickled Garlic, Turnips and Cucumbers

The Jewish side of my family loves crunchy, garlicky cucumber pickles. Turnips add a whole new look to this traditional recipe, adapted from Lloyd J. Harris's The Book of Garlic. *Pickled garlic is not as potent as fresh; toss the whole cloves into a salad dressed with a slightly sweet vinaigrette.*

2 pounds pickling cucumbers, trimmed
2 pounds baby turnips, trimmed
2 large whole garlic bulbs, cloves separated and
    peeled, or 10 to 12 pearl onions, peeled
3 to 4 large sprigs fresh dill
2 quarts water
2 bay leaves
1/4 cup (2 ounces) kosher salt
1/2 cup (4 ounces) pickling spices
1/2 cup granulated sugar
4 or 5 fresh cayenne hot red chili peppers (optional)

In a large, wide-mouthed ceramic or glass crock, layer the cucumbers, turnips, garlic cloves or pearl onions, and dill. In a saucepan, bring the water to a boil. Add the bay leaves, salt, pickling spices, sugar, and the chili peppers if you want spicy pickles. Stir to dissolve the salt and sugar. Pour the hot brine over the vegetables, covering completely. Using a plate and a heavy object (try a large can of food or a clean brick), weight down the vegetables to keep them immersed in the brine and cover with a cloth. Cure in the refrigerator or in a cool place for about 1 week.

    Transfer the pickles to sterilized pint jars, pour in the brine to cover, cap tightly and store in the refrigerator for up to 6 months. *Makes 5 or 6 pints*

Sweet and Spicy Red Onion Marmalade

This recipe has endless possibilities. Serve it warm as a sauce over smoked chicken or chilled, paired with cream cheese on top of a toasted onion bagel.

1 tablespoon olive oil
3 medium-sized red onions, finely chopped
2 or 3 fresh jalapeño or other hot chili peppers,
    seeded and minced
1/4 cup dry-packed sun-dried tomatoes, minced
1 tart cooking apple, such as Granny Smith or
    pippin, quartered, cored, peeled and grated
1/2 cup golden raisins, chopped
3/4 cup red wine vinegar
1 cup firmly packed brown sugar
1 cinnamon stick
1 cup apple juice or water
Salt, to taste

In a large, heavy-bottomed saucepan over medium-low heat, warm the oil. Add the onions and chilies and sauté for approximately 45 minutes, or until the onions are soft.

    Add all the remaining ingredients except the salt. Place over low heat and bring to a gentle simmer. Cook, uncovered, for approximately 1 hour, or until all the ingredients are soft and the marmalade begins to thicken. Stir frequently. If all the moisture has evaporated but the onions aren't fully cooked, add more water and continue to cook until the mixture is reduced to a thick, jamlike consistency.

    Remove from the heat. Season with salt. You may choose to add more chili pepper at this time. Store in the refrigerator for up to 2 weeks. *Makes approximately 2 pints*

Spicy Green Onion Corn Muffins

These muffins are moist and flavorful and make a splendid addition to a breakfast of chorizo, scrambled eggs and salsa.

1 cup buttermilk
1/4 cup firmly packed brown sugar
1/4 cup sour cream
1 egg
1/4 cup vegetable oil
3/4 cup blue or yellow medium-grind cornmeal
1 1/4 cups unbleached white flour
2 teaspoons baking powder
1/2 teaspoon baking soda
1/4 teaspoon salt
1 tablespoon pure ground chili powder (ancho or chipotle)
1/3 cup finely chopped green onion, including tender green tops
1/4 cup grated red onion
3/4 cup grated Monterey Jack cheese
1/2 cup chopped fresh cilantro

Preheat the oven to 400 degrees F. Oil a standard 12-cup muffin tin (or two 6-cup tins).

In a large bowl, beat together the buttermilk, brown sugar, sour cream, egg and oil until well blended. In a medium-sized bowl, stir together the cornmeal, flour, baking powder, baking soda, salt and chili powder. Gradually add the flour mixture to the buttermilk mixture, stirring until blended. Fold in the green onion, red onion, cheese and cilantro. Divide the batter among the muffin cups, filling each one three-fourths full.

Bake for approximately 15 minutes, or until browned and firm to the touch. Let cool in the pan briefly, then turn out of the pan. Serve warm. *Makes 12 muffins*

Left to right: Spicy Green Onion Corn Muffins, Onion Confit Overnight Breakfast Rolls (recipe p. 54) and Winter Squash and Onion Cheddar Torta (recipe p. 56)

Onion Confit Overnight Breakfast Rolls

I love this breakfast roll recipe because almost all the work takes place the night before.
The dough rises in the refrigerator while you sleep, and in the morning the elements come together in no time
at all, baking into light, tender rolls. If you have adventurous eaters who don't mind garlic for breakfast,
cook a few cloves into the confit. Serve the rolls with sweet butter and cups of dark rich coffee.

Dough:
1/4 cup (1/2 stick) unsalted butter, melted
1/2 cup milk
1 tablespoon granulated sugar
1 egg, lightly beaten
2 1/4 cups unbleached white flour
1 package (scant 1 tablespoon) active dry yeast
3/4 teaspoon salt
1/2 teaspoon freshly ground black pepper

Confit:
1 tablespoon unsalted butter
1 tablespoon olive oil
2 pounds onions (preferably fall/storage) or shallots,
    thinly sliced
4 cloves garlic, thinly sliced (optional)
Pinch of salt

Egg Wash:
1 egg yolk
1 tablespoon water

To make the dough, in a small saucepan over low heat, combine the butter, milk and sugar and heat until the butter is melted. Cool to approximately 120 degrees F.

While the butter is melting, in a large mixing bowl, or in the bowl of an electric mixer fitted with the paddle attachment, combine the egg, flour, yeast, salt and pepper. Gradually add the warm liquid to the dry ingredients while beating with a spoon or the paddle attachment. Continue to beat for approximately 3 minutes, or until the mixture forms a soft dough. Transfer to a clean bowl, cover and refrigerate overnight.

To make the confit, in a heavy-bottomed sauté pan over low heat, melt the butter with the oil. Add the onions or shallots, and the garlic if using, and sauté until very soft, approximately 40 minutes to 1 hour. Season with salt, let cool, cover and refrigerate.

In the morning, preheat the oven to 375 degrees F. Lightly oil a baking sheet.

Turn out the dough onto a lightly floured work surface and divide into 3 equal pieces. Roll out each piece into a round that is approximately 1/8 inch thick. Cover each round with one-third of the confit. Cut each round into 4 equal wedges.

To make the rolls, begin at the wide end of each wedge and roll up the wedge, ending with the point visible. Place pointed side down on a lightly oiled baking sheet. Repeat until all of the rolls are formed, and then let them sit for approximately 15 minutes.

In a small bowl, whisk together the egg yolk and water. Brush the tops of the rolls generously with the egg wash. Bake for approximately 12 minutes, or until golden brown. Serve warm. *Makes 12 rolls*

Left to right: Spicy Green Onion Corn Muffins (recipe p. 53) and Onion Confit Overnight Breakfast Rolls

Winter Squash and Onion Cheddar Torta

*When I have guests for the night, I love to serve them a simple breakfast of warm biscuits,
juicy orange wedges and this breakfast torta. All of the ingredients can be prepared the night before and
then assembled that morning, giving you more time to enjoy conversation with your friends.*

10 eggs
1 cup sour cream
3/4 cup milk
1/4 cup chopped fresh parsley
3 tablespoons olive oil, or more if needed
1 large yellow onion (preferably fall/storage),
    thinly sliced
3 cups diced cooked pumpkin, butternut or other
    dense winter squash (1/2-inch dice)

1 1/2 teaspoons salt
1 teaspoon freshly ground black pepper
5 ounces aged cheddar cheese, cut into
    1/4-inch dice
1/4 cup freshly grated Parmesan cheese
Homemade or store-bought pesto, for garnish
    (optional)

Preheat the oven to 400 degrees F.

In a bowl, whisk together the eggs, sour cream, milk and parsley. Set aside.

In a large cast-iron or other ovenproof, heavy-bottomed skillet, warm 3 tablespoons of olive oil over medium heat. Add the onion and sauté for approximately 5 minutes, or until softened. Add the squash and continue cooking, stirring frequently until fully heated through. Season with the salt and pepper.

Be sure the sides of the skillet are coated with oil, adding a few tablespoons of oil if necessary. Also, check that the ingredients in the skillet are very hot. Then pour the egg mixture over the squash and onion. Scatter the cheddar cheese evenly over the top, pushing the pieces down into the batter so that they are covered. Sprinkle the surface evenly with the Parmesan.

Place the skillet in the oven and immediately reduce the oven temperature to 375 degrees F. Bake 30 to 45 minutes, or until the center puffs up slightly and is firm to the touch. Remove from the oven and let stand for 5 to 10 minutes, then cut into wedges to serve. Garnish with pesto, if desired. *Serves 6*

Chive Rice Pancakes with Green Onion and Melon Salsa

Once the rice is cooked, these crisp pancakes come together relatively easily. The green onions
bridge the toasty character of sesame oil with the refreshing quality of melon. Serve the pancakes topped
with the relish at a summer barbecue to accompany grilled tuna, swordfish or salmon.

Rice Pancakes:
2 teaspoons sesame seeds
2 cups cooked white rice, at room temperature
2 tablespoons finely chopped garlic chives
1 or 2 eggs
2 to 3 teaspoons Asian sesame oil
1/2 teaspoon salt, or to taste

Green Onion and Melon Salsa:
2 cups peeled, seeded and cubed melon (2/3-inch cubes)
1/4 cup finely chopped green onion tops
1/4 cup chopped fresh cilantro
2 tablespoons mirin (Japanese sweet wine; optional)
1 teaspoon finely chopped fresh hot red chili pepper,
*   such as cayenne or jalapeño, or to taste*

Canola or vegetable oil, for frying

To make the rice pancakes, in a small, dry skillet over low heat, toast the sesame seeds until lightly golden. Set aside.

In a medium-sized bowl, combine the rice, chives and 1 egg. Using your hands, mix the ingredients together. Add the sesame seeds and 2 teaspoons sesame oil and mix well. Season with salt and more sesame oil to taste. Add another egg if the batter is not the consistency of a thick pancake batter. Set aside.

To make the salsa, in a small bowl, toss together the melon cubes, green onion tops, cilantro, *mirin* and chili. Let stand at room temperature while you fry the rice cakes. *Makes approximately 3 cups*

In a heavy-bottomed skillet, pour in oil to a depth of 1/16 inch and heat just until it begins to smoke. When the oil is hot, working in batches, spoon about 1/4 cup of the rice mixture into the skillet to form each pancake. Using a large spoon or a spatula, press against the pancakes to flatten them slightly. Fry, turning once, for approximately 3 minutes, or until browned and crispy on both sides. Using a slotted utensil, transfer to paper towels to drain. Keep warm in a low oven while you cook the remaining pancakes.

Serve the pancakes hot. Generously top them with the relish. *Makes 8 to 10 pancakes; serves 4 or 5*

Tempura Onion Rings with Korean Hot Sauce

*There are two onion ring recipes in this book. The onion strings (recipe p. 70) are delicate and crispy.
But these rings, made from thick slices of succulent sweet onions, are the kind I remember getting at the diner
in my hometown, before the advent of frozen foods. We ate them smothered in catsup or gravy.
Nowadays, I enjoy them with just a sprinkle of salt or dipped into this tasty, low-fat hot sauce. For this dish
to be at its best, the water that goes into the batter must be very cold. If you haven't time for the water to
become ice cold, drop an ice cube and another 1 tablespoon of flour into the batter.*

2 large yellow or white onions (preferably
    spring/summer), cut into thick slices or wedges
Cold water
Peanut oil, for deep-frying

Hot Sauce:
1/3 cup soy sauce
2 tablespoons mirin (Japanese sweet cooking wine)
1 teaspoon chopped fresh ginger
1 teaspoon chopped garlic

1 tablespoon brown sugar
1/2 teaspoon red pepper flakes
2 tablespoons chopped fresh chives

Batter:
1 cup unbleached white flour
2 tablespoons cornstarch
1 egg
1 cup ice water

In a large bowl or other container, combine the onions and cold water to cover. Let stand while you prepare the rest of the ingredients.

In a heavy-bottomed saucepan or an electric fryer, pour in oil to a depth of 3 to 4 inches and heat until it begins to smoke.

While the oil is heating, in a small bowl, combine all the ingredients for the hot sauce and stir well. Set aside.

Assemble all the ingredients for the batter. Then, just before you are ready to begin frying the onions, in a small bowl, stir together the flour and cornstarch. In a medium-sized bowl, using a fork, whisk together the egg and ice water until blended. Add the flour mixture to the egg mixture and whisk just until combined. The batter should be slightly lumpy.

When the oil is hot, drain the onion rings. Dip them, a few at a time, into the batter, shaking off any excess, and then slip them into the oil. If the batter is not sticking to the onions before you add them to the oil, add a bit more flour to the batter. Fry for 3 to 5 minutes, or until golden brown. Using large slotted spoon, remove to paper towels to drain. Keep the onion rings warm until all of them are cooked. Arrange the onion rings on a platter and sprinkle with salt, if you like. Serve with the hot sauce. *Serves 4*

Grilled Red Onions and Green Tomatoes with Rosemary Aioli

Even before it was fashionable, my father cooked vegetables on the grill right next to the steaks. On our picnic table, which sat beneath a giant maple tree, we would find big platters of whatever came from his garden, my favorite being the harvest of onions and green tomatoes. If you are afraid that the onion slices will fall apart on the grill without support, soak bamboo skewers (two for each onion slice) in water to cover for 30 minutes, drain, and then run the skewers through the center of the slice, to form a cross.

Rosemary Aioli:
1 egg yolk
Juice of 1/2 lemon
2 or 3 cloves garlic, minced
2 tablespoons finely chopped fresh rosemary
2 tablespoons grated lemon zest
1 cup extra virgin olive oil
Salt and freshly ground black pepper, to taste

Marinade:
1/3 cup extra virgin olive oil

3 cloves garlic, minced
1/2 cup finely chopped fresh basil
2 tablespoons finely chopped fresh oregano
3 tablespoons red wine vinegar
Salt and freshly ground black pepper, to taste

2 medium-sized red, yellow or white onions
(spring/summer or freshly picked fall/storage),
cut into slices 1/2 to 1 inch thick
2 or 3 green tomatoes, cut into slices 1/2 inch thick
Lemon wedges, for serving

To make the aioli by hand, in a bowl, whisk together the egg yolk, lemon juice, garlic, rosemary and lemon zest. Drop by drop, add the olive oil, whisking constantly. When the mixture begins to thicken and emulsify, begin adding the oil a little more quickly, but always in a very fine stream. When all of the oil has been added and the mixture is the consistency of mayonnaise, season with salt and pepper.

To make the aioli in a food processor or blender, combine all the ingredients except the oil and salt and pepper in the container and blend until thoroughly combined. With the motor running, add the olive oil, first drop by drop and then in a very slow, steady stream and continue processing until the mixture is the consistency of mayonnaise. Season with salt and pepper. Cover and refrigerate until serving (or for up to 5 days). You will have approximately 1 cup.

Prepare a charcoal fire in a grill. While waiting for the fire to burn down, make the marinade. In a shallow bowl, whisk together all the marinade ingredients.

When the coals are medium-hot, dip the onion and tomato slices, one at a time, into the marinade and place on the grill. Cook, turning often so that they cook slowly rather than burn. They should be ready in 8 to 10 minutes.

Place the onions and tomatoes on a platter. Serve the aioli and lemon wedges in separate bowls alongside. *Serves 4 to 6*

Spicy Purple Cabbage Salad with Ginger, Papaya, Pomegranate and Chives

Purple cabbage is a regal feast for the eyes when used as a backdrop for this combination of papaya, pomegranate and chives. I love to include this sprightly creation as a spicy side dish for a Christmas feast. You can substitute green onion tops in place of the chives.

1 medium-sized head purple cabbage, cored and
   very thinly sliced
1/2 bunch fresh chives, chopped, plus chopped fresh
   chives, for garnish
1/2 cup brown sugar
3/4 cup seasoned rice wine vinegar
1 teaspoon salt
1/2 teaspoon or more red pepper flakes
3 tablespoons grated fresh ginger
1 1/2 cups peeled, seeded and diced papaya
   (1-inch cubes)
Seeds of 1 pomegranate

In a large bowl, toss together the cabbage, the chopped chives, sugar, vinegar, salt, pepper flakes and ginger. Allow to stand at room temperature for 30 minutes to an hour, stirring every 10 minutes to blend the flavors.

Add the papaya to the cabbage mixture and toss to mix. Transfer to a large serving bowl or platter. Garnish with the pomegranate seeds and more chives. *Serves 6 to 8*

Baked Yams with Green Onion and Berry Butter

This colorful way of dressing up a yam or sweet potato is wonderful alongside a thick-cut pork chop or smoky ham slice. Finish the plate with a sprinkling of whole berries.

4 medium-sized garnet yams or sweet potatoes
Canola or vegetable oil
1/2 cup (1 stick) unsalted butter, at room temperature
2 small green onions, including tender green tops,
   finely chopped, plus small whole green onions,
   for garnish
1/2 small basket very sweet, ripe raspberries or
   blackberries, plus a few berries, for garnish
2 tablespoons brown sugar
1 to 2 teaspoons crème de cassis
1 teaspoon salt, or to taste
1/2 teaspoon freshly ground black pepper

Preheat the oven to 375 degrees F.

Lightly coat the yams or sweet potatoes with oil. Bake for approximately 45 minutes, or until soft when pierced.

Meanwhile, in a bowl, combine the butter, chopped green onion, berries, brown sugar, crème de cassis, salt and pepper. Using an electric mixer or a spoon, mix until well blended.

When the yams or sweet potatoes are ready, remove from the oven and split them open. Spoon an equal portion of the butter mixture onto each yam. Serve immediately. *Serves 4*

Leek, Onion and Mushroom Stock

Fat-free and full of vitamins, vegetable stock can be used in place of meat stock in many recipes.
I suggest making a big batch and then freezing it in several small lock-top plastic bags or ice-cube trays
to have on hand whenever you need to add oomph to a roast, stew or soup. In my opinion,
the more onions and leeks in a stock, the better it is, so measure generously.

6 large leeks, including green tops
1 large yellow or white onion (preferably fall/
    storage), skin intact
1 large fennel bulb, or 5 celery stalks
1 pound fresh shiitake mushrooms
1/2 pound domestic mushrooms
2 large carrots
2 whole garlic bulbs, broken into cloves, unpeeled

1 bunch fresh thyme or sage
1 bunch fresh parsley
Big handful of dry-packed sun-dried tomatoes
1 can (15 ounces) tomatoes, or 3 large fresh
    ripe tomatoes
1 cup full-bodied red wine, such as a Cabernet or
    Zinfandel (optional)
Salt and freshly ground black pepper, to taste

Clean all the vegetables and herbs and chop coarsely. Then, in a large pot, combine all the ingredients except the salt and pepper. Cover generously with water and bring to a boil. Reduce the heat to low and simmer, uncovered, for 3 or 4 hours, or until the liquid has reduced and the flavors from the vegetables have been imparted to the stock.

Strain the stock through a sieve, discarding the vegetables. Then strain the stock again, this time through a fine-mesh sieve lined with cheesecloth to remove any sediment. Season with plenty of salt and pepper and store in tightly capped jars in the refrigerator for up to 1 week or in the freezer for 4 to 6 months, as described above. *Makes 2 to 3 quarts*

MAIN COURSES

Onions, which have traditionally been used as a seasoning or a bit player in a side dish, have found their way to the heart of the meal in this chapter, taking their place center stage. And while we may think of onion rings as an appetizer or as something to accompany a hamburger, here frilly onion strings become the leading player when generously nested beneath a crisp game hen.

In Lamb Shanks and Shallots with Juniper Berry Sauce, shallots are first cooked down to season the sauce. Then along with potatoes and carrots, more shallots are roasted whole, to be relished as an unforgettable vegetable.

There are a number of addictive dishes in this chapter, many of which are recipes taken from the fifties and sixties and infused with a new oniony twist. Caramelized onions transform down-home meat loaf into an utterly contemporary dinner. A traditional shepherd's pie has been revamped into a meatless dish that mixes sautéed leeks into the potato crown. And chives or chive blossoms bring new life to the old standby of mashed potatoes, served under grilled salmon.

Asparagus spears are spring vegetables and so are sweet onions, so it seems natural to team up the two in the enticing Leek, Ham and Asparagus Gratin. Equally complementary are mild spring onions and crisp bacon, here paired in a scrumptious Sweet Onion, Olive and Bacon Tart.

Sweet Onion, Olive and Bacon Tart

I like to use mild spring onions for this recipe because they offer a gentle onion flavor and a bit more texture when lightly baked. In summer, serve the tart next to slices of multicolored vine-ripened tomatoes.

Tart Shell:
2 1/2 cups unbleached white flour
2 tablespoons chopped fresh thyme
1/2 teaspoon salt
1 cup (2 sticks) chilled unsalted butter,
*   cut into 8 equal pieces*
2/3 cup sour cream

Filling:
4 slices bacon
3 tablespoons olive oil
1 1/2 pounds yellow or white (preferably spring/
*   summer onions), very thinly sliced*
3/4 cup chopped, pitted Kalamata olives
Generous grating of fresh nutmeg
Salt and freshly ground black pepper, to taste

To make the tart shell in a food processor, combine the flour, thyme and salt and process to mix. Add the butter and process until the mixture is mealy. Spoon the sour cream in dollops around the sides of the processor bowl and process, using the pulse button, just until a firm ball gathers around the blade.

To make the tart shell by hand, in a bowl, stir together the flour, thyme and salt. Add the butter and, using a pastry blender or 2 knives, cut in the butter until the mixture is mealy. Add the sour cream and, using a fork or your hands, mix it in until a rough mass forms. Form the dough into a ball.

Remove the ball from the processor or bowl to a lightly floured work surface and divide in half. Pat each half into an oval. Wrap one half securely in plastic wrap and refrigerate or freeze for up to 1 week for later use. Roll out the other half into a round 12 to 14 inches in diameter and 1/8 inch thick. Transfer the round to a lightly floured baking sheet or pizza pan. Cover and refrigerate until needed.

To make the filling, in a large, heavy-bottomed sauté pan over medium heat, fry the bacon until crisp. Using tongs or a slotted spoon, remove to paper towels to drain. Discard the bacon fat. Crumble the bacon into bite-sized pieces.

In the same pan, warm the olive oil over low heat. Add the onions and sauté for 30 to 45 minutes, or until soft. Stir in the olives and bacon and season with nutmeg, salt and freshly ground pepper. Remove from the heat and let cool to room temperature.

Preheat the oven to 375 degrees F.

Remove the dough round from the refrigerator. Spread the onion mixture evenly over the crust, leaving a 2-inch border uncovered (or more than 2 inches if you want to fold more of the crust over). Fold the uncovered crust over the onions.

Bake for approximately 30 minutes, or until the crust browns. Remove from the oven and let stand for 15 minutes. Serve warm or at room temperature, cut into wedges. *Serves 6*

Roasted Game Hens with
Honey Mustard Sauce on an Onion String Nest

The crisp and light onion strings that form a nest for the hens are
delicious all by themselves. They become even more tempting, however, when
paired with bites of game hen cloaked in a sweet, spicy mustard sauce.

Game Hens:
4 Cornish game hens
1 lemon, quartered
4 sprigs fresh thyme or sage
8 cloves garlic
Olive oil
Salt and freshly ground black pepper, to taste

Onion Strings:
2 cups unbleached white flour
1/4 cup cornstarch
2 teaspoons dried thyme
1/2 teaspoon salt
1 teaspoon freshly ground black pepper
2 large yellow, white or red onions
Ice water, to cover
Peanut oil, for deep-frying

Honey Mustard Sauce:
Approximately 1 cup chicken stock or water
Reserved pan juices from game hens
Approximately 1/2 cup chicken stock, or as needed
2 tablespoons unsalted butter
3 tablespoons unbleached flour
1 tablespoon dried thyme
2 tablespoons Dijon mustard
1 tablespoon honey
1 tablespoon dry white wine

Preheat the oven to 450 degrees F.

Remove any body parts from the cavity of each game hen, wash thoroughly inside and out, and pat dry. Fill each cavity with a lemon quarter, 1 herb sprig and 2 garlic cloves. Lightly oil the skin of the hens and season with salt and pepper. Place in a roasting pan.

Place the pan in the oven and immediately reduce the oven temperature to 350 degrees F. Bake for approximately 45 minutes, or until an instant-read thermometer inserted into a thigh joint away from the bone registers 160 degrees F. or the juices run clear when pierced at the thigh joint.

Meanwhile, to ready the onions for cooking, in a medium-sized bowl, stir together the flour, cornstarch, thyme, salt and pepper. Very thinly slice the onions. (If you have a mandoline, use it, as it produces the thinnest possible slices.) In another bowl, combine the onions and ice water to cover.

In a wide, heavy-bottomed saucepan or deep skillet, pour in oil to a depth of 3 to 4 inches. Set aside.

Transfer the cooked hens to a platter and keep warm. To make the sauce, pour 1/2 cup water or chicken stock into the roasting pan.

Stir well, collecting all the juices and fat in the pan. Strain through a fine-mesh sieve into a measuring cup. Add enough additional stock or water to measure 1 cup. Set aside.

In a small saucepan over medium heat, melt the butter. When it foams, add the flour and cook, stirring constantly, for 3 to 4 minutes. Gradually add the reserved pan juices and stock mixture, stirring constantly. Stir in the thyme, mustard, honey and white wine until fully incorporated. Continue to cook for a few more minutes until the sauce thickens. Cover and keep warm over low heat.

Meanwhile, to cook the onion strings, heat the oil until it just begins to smoke. When the oil is hot, drain the onions and toss them in the flour mixture to coat and shake off excess. Working in batches, drop them by small handfuls into the oil and fry for 3 to 4 minutes, or until golden brown. Using a slotted spoon or tongs, remove to paper towels to drain.

Create a nest of the fried onion strings on 4 individual plates. Place a warm hen in the center of each nest. Pour an equal amount of the honey mustard sauce evenly over each hen and serve immediately. *Serves 4*

Leek, Ham and Asparagus Gratin

I know spring has arrived when asparagus and baby leeks show up in the market. As the season moves on, the stalks grow thicker, the flavors deepen, and the vegetables better lend themselves to casseroles and gratins.

1 pound medium-sized asparagus stalks
8 to 10 small young leeks or large bunching onions
Ice water, to cover
1 tablespoon unsalted butter, plus 1/4 cup
    (1/2 stick) unsalted butter, melted
1/2 pound fresh domestic or wild mushrooms,
    brushed clean, tough stems removed, and cut
    into 1/4-inch thick slices
1 tablespoon chopped fresh chives
1 tablespoon chopped fresh marjoram

2 tablespoons chopped fresh parsley
2 tablespoons dry white wine
4 eggs
1 1/2 to 2 cups milk
1/2 teaspoon salt
1/2 teaspoon white pepper
Pinch of ground cloves
6 to 8 thick slices sweet Italian bread
1/3 pound cooked ham, thinly sliced
4 to 6 ounces Jarlsberg cheese, grated

Preheat the oven to 375 degrees F.

Typically, spring asparagus and leeks have no tough parts, but if they do, remove them from both. Rinse the asparagus and leeks thoroughly. Cut the asparagus and leeks into 1-inch pieces. Ready a large bowl of ice water. Bring a medium-sized saucepan three-fourths full of water to a boil. Add the asparagus and parboil until half-cooked. The timing will depend upon the thickness of the stalks; pierce with a knife to test. Using a slotted spoon or tongs, transfer the asparagus to the ice water to stop the cooking.

Add the leeks to the boiling water and boil until half-cooked. Again, the timing will depend upon the thickness of the stalks; pierce to test. Drain and add to the ice water to stop the cooking. Then drain both the asparagus and leeks and set aside.

In a small sauté pan over medium heat, melt 1 tablespoon of butter. Add the mushrooms, chives, marjoram and parsley and sauté for approximately 5 minutes, or until they just begin to soften. Add the wine and deglaze the pan, stirring to release any bits stuck to the bottom. Remove from the heat and set aside.

In a medium-sized bowl, whisk together the eggs, milk, salt, pepper and cloves; set aside. Arrange half of the bread in a single layer in the bottom of a 4-quart baking dish with 4-inch sides. Pour half of the melted butter evenly over the bread. Cover the bread with half of the asparagus spears and leeks. Top with half of the ham and then half of the sautéed mushrooms. Repeat the layers. Pour the milk mixture evenly over everything. Push down lightly with the back of a large spoon, so both layers of bread are soaked with the milk mixture. Sprinkle the cheese over the top.

Bake for 45 minutes to 1 hour, or until the top is browned and the center is firm to the touch. Allow to sit at room temperature for 15 minutes before serving. Using a spoon, scoop out onto individual plates. *Serves 4 to 6*

Stuffed Roasted Chicken with
Braised Green Garlic and Garlic Bruschetta

Green garlic, whether chopped and added to salad greens, tossed at the last minute into a bowl of basmati rice or braised with chicken, is one of my favorite ways to welcome spring. If you cannot find green garlic bulbs to make this dish, green onions or baby leeks can be used in their place.

Basting Mixture:
1/4 cup extra virgin olive oil
4 cloves garlic, minced
Salt and freshly ground black pepper, to taste

Chicken and Green Garlic:
2 small chickens (2 to 2 1/2 pounds each),
    split in half
Salt and freshly ground black pepper, to taste
1 tablespoon unsalted butter
16 green garlic bulbs or baby leeks, with greens intact
1 or 2 bay leaves
5 pink peppercorns, coarsely crushed
1 or 2 carrots, sliced into 3-inch-long julienne
Leaves from 10 fresh chervil sprigs

1 tablespoon grated lemon zest
Juice of 1 lemon
5 cloves garlic, minced
1 1/2 cups chicken stock

Goat Cheese Stuffing:
4 ounces soft fresh goat cheese
1 tablespoon grated red onion
1/2 teaspoon freshly ground black pepper
1 to 2 teaspoons chopped fresh sage
1 to 2 tablespoons chopped pesticide-free geranium
    blossoms (optional)

4 thick hand-cut slices country-style whole-wheat or
    white bread

Preheat the oven to 400 degrees F.

To make the basting mixture, in a bowl, stir together the olive oil, garlic and a generous amount of salt and pepper. Let stand at room temperature for 15 minutes.

To ready the halved chickens for roasting, rub them lightly with some of the basting mixture. Reserve the remaining mixture for using on the bruschetta. Generously salt and pepper the skin. Place the chickens on a baking sheet, skin side up, and roast for approximately 45 minutes, or until an instant-read thermometer inserted into the thigh joint away from the bone registers 160 degrees F., or the juices run clear when pierced at a thigh joint. Remove

the chickens and let them cool until they can be handled. Using your hands, carefully pull away the breastbones.

While the chickens are cooking, in a heavy-bottomed pan over medium-low heat, melt the butter. Add the green garlic or leeks and sauté for approximately 10 minutes, or until lightly browned. Add the bay leaves, pink peppercorns, carrots, chervil, lemon zest and juice, minced garlic and chicken stock. Simmer, uncovered, over medium-high heat for 25 to 40 minutes, or until the green garlic and carrots are soft and the stock has reduced by about one-third. Remove the bay leaves and discard. Season with salt.

To make the stuffing, in a small bowl, stir together the goat cheese, red onion, black pepper, sage, and the geranium blossoms, if using, until well blended.

Loosen the skin covering the breast and thigh of each chicken half, being careful not to tear it. Gently stuff one-fourth of the cheese mixture evenly under the skin of each. Flatten the skin to its original shape as much as possible.

Preheat the broiler. To make the bruschetta, generously brush one side of each bread slice with the remaining basting mixture and place on a broiler pan, oiled side up. Broil for a few minutes until lightly browned. Set aside.

Reduce the oven temperature to 375 degrees F. Return the chicken to the oven for approximately 10 minutes, or until warmed throughout. At the same time, reheat the green garlic and carrot mixture.

To serve, place a piece of the toasted bread on each plate. Lean a chicken half atop each slice. Smother each chicken half with the braised green garlic and carrot mixture. Serve immediately. *Serves 4*

Green Onion and Dungeness Crab Fritters
with Spicy Tartar Sauce

Substitute corn kernels or peas for the crab if you're on a tight budget or if you can't eat seafood.
Plain green-onion fritters and the spicy tartar sauce would be good served alongside scrambled eggs for brunch.
The fritter batter can be made a few hours in advance, as it holds up beautifully in the refrigerator.

Tartar Sauce:
1 cup homemade mayonnaise
2 tablespoons grated red onion
2 tablespoons drained capers
2 tablespoons bottled grated horseradish
2 tablespoons fresh lemon juice
1 tablespoon chopped fresh parsley
1 tablespoon Dijon mustard
Tabasco sauce or other hot-pepper sauce, to taste
Dash of Worcestershire sauce

Fritters:
2 tablespoons unbleached white flour
1/2 teaspoon baking powder
1/2 teaspoon salt
1/8 teaspoon white pepper
3 eggs, lightly beaten
1 teaspoon finely chopped garlic
1 cup finely chopped green onions
1 1/2 cups freshly cooked Dungeness crab meat
1 teaspoon finely chopped fresh ginger (optional)
Peanut oil, for frying

To make the tartar sauce, in a small bowl, stir together the mayonnaise, red onion, capers, horseradish, lemon juice, parsley and mustard until well mixed. Add the Tabasco and Worcestershire sauces. Cover and refrigerate until using.

To make the fritters, in a medium-sized bowl, stir together the flour, baking powder, salt and white pepper. Stir in the eggs, garlic, green onions, crab meat and the ginger, if using, until well blended.

In a heavy-bottomed skillet, pour in oil to a depth of 1/2 inch and heat just until it begins to smoke. When the oil is ready, drop the fritter batter by large spoonfuls into the oil. Cook, turning once, for approximately 3 minutes on each side, or until browned and cooked through. Using a slotted spoon or spatula, transfer the fritters to paper towels to drain briefly. Keep warm in a low oven.

Arrange the fritters on a platter. Serve immediately with the tartar sauce on the side.
Serves 6

Angel Hair Pasta with Garlic Shrimp, Nasturtiums and Green Onions

This pasta dish takes about half an hour to prepare. The green onions bring together all the other flavors. The nasturtium leaves add a peppery quality, and the bright orange and yellow blossoms turn a relatively easy dish into a celebration. Be sure to use only pesticide-free flowers and leaves. If you can't find nasturtiums, you will still have a delicious pasta dish.

1/4 cup (1/2 stick) unsalted butter
3 tablespoons virgin olive oil
1 tablespoon chopped garlic
2 tablespoons chopped fresh ginger
1 teaspoon paprika
1/2 to 1 teaspoon Tabasco sauce or
    other hot-pepper sauce

1/2 cup Champagne, or as needed
1 bunch green onions, including tender green tops,
    thinly sliced
1 1/2 pounds shrimp, peeled and deveined
12 large nasturtium leaves, thinly sliced
1 pound angel hair pasta
12 nasturtium blossoms, for garnish

Bring a large pot three-fourths full of salted water to a boil.

Meanwhile, in a large sauté pan over medium heat, melt the butter and add the olive oil, garlic, ginger, paprika and Tabasco. Add the 1/2 cup Champagne, green onions, shrimp and the nasturtium leaves. Watching closely, and tossing every now and then, heat just until the shrimp turn pink and curl into half moons. This will take approximately 5 minutes. (Overcooking will make the shrimp rubbery and dry.) If the pan begins to dry out, add a little more Champagne as needed to moisten.

While the shrimp are cooking, drop the angel hair pasta into the boiling water and cook until al dente. Check the package directions for timing; do not overcook.

Drain the pasta and divide among 4 dinner plates. Spoon one-fourth of the shrimp sauce over each serving. Garnish with whole nasturtium blossoms or remove the petals and toss randomly over each serving. *Serves 4*

Chive Ricotta Gnocchi with Garlic and Sage Brown Butter

A dish of gnocchi is one of my favorite meals. Flavoring the dough with chives and then finishing the cooked gnocchi with a nutty brown garlic butter is my idea of real eating.

Gnocchi:
1 pound ricotta cheese
2 egg whites
1/2 cup finely chopped fresh chives or
    green onion tops
1 1/4 to 1 1/2 cups unbleached white flour
1 teaspoon salt
1/2 teaspoon freshly ground black pepper

Garlic and Sage Brown Butter:
1/3 cup unsalted butter
6 large cloves garlic, chopped coarsely
Leaves from 1 bunch fresh sage
Salt and freshly ground black pepper, to taste

2 tablespoons chopped fresh chives, for garnish
Freshly grated Parmesan cheese, for garnish

To make the gnocchi, in a large mixing bowl, combine the ricotta, egg whites and chives or green onions and mix well. In a medium-sized bowl, combine the 1 1/4 cups flour, salt and pepper. Gradually add the dry ingredients to the ricotta mixture, folding just until blended. Add as much of the remaining 1/4 cup flour as needed to form a dough that is moist yet not too sticky.

Turn out the dough onto a lightly floured work surface and divide into 4 balls. Using your palms, roll each ball against the work surface into a rope approximately 1/2 inch in diameter. Try not to overwork the dough or work too much flour into it, or it will toughen. Using a sharp knife, cut off 1-inch pieces. Using the tines of a fork, flatten each piece, imprinting the tines in the surface. As the gnocchi are formed, place them on a flour-dusted baking sheet. (At this point, the gnocchi can be covered and refrigerated for up to 2 days or frozen for up to 2 months. To freeze, place the baking sheet in the freezer; when the gnocchi are frozen solid, transfer them to lock-top bags and return to the freezer.)

Bring a large pot three-fourths full of water to a boil.

While the water is heating, in a sauté pan over medium heat, warm the butter until it begins to brown. Add the garlic and sage leaves and sauté for approximately 3 minutes, or until the garlic is soft and the butter is browned but not burned. Season with salt and pepper. Keep warm.

Drop the gnocchi into the boiling water. They are cooked when they float to the surface. This will take 3 to 5 minutes. Meanwhile, reheat the browned butter, if necessary. Drain the gnocchi and place in a warmed serving dish. Pour the browned butter over the top and toss to coat. Garnish with the chives and grated cheese and serve immediately. *Serves 4*

Grilled Salmon on Chive Blossom Mashed Potatoes

If I were to put a descriptive culinary label on the early nineties, it would be The Mashed Potato Era. An unstable economic environment sent many of us back to the basics, searching for sensible foods to fill our bodies and souls. Food professionals have a tendency to take everything a step or two further, which is how these luscious mashed potatoes came to be. If you like, pan-sear rather than grill the salmon fillets.

1/2 cup crème fraîche
3 tablespoons seeded and grated cucumber
2 tablespoons grated red onion
2 tablespoons dry vermouth
Salt and freshly ground black pepper, to taste
Approximately 3 pounds medium-sized russet
    potatoes, peeled and cut lengthwise into quarters
1/4 cup (1/2 stick) unsalted butter, cut into
    small pieces

6 generous tablespoons sour cream
Milk, for thinning, if needed
2 to 3 tablespoons garlic or regular chive blossom
    petals, plus additional blossoms for garnish
White pepper, to taste
Clarified butter, melted
4 salmon fillets (7 or 8 ounces each)
4 teaspoons caviar or 8 teaspoons chopped black
    olives (optional)

In a small bowl, combine the crème fraîche, cucumber, red onion and vermouth. Season with salt and black pepper and set aside to allow the flavors to blend.

Prepare a mesquite fire in a grill.

While the fire is reaching the proper heat, bring a large saucepan three-fourths full of water to a boil. Add the potatoes and boil for 15 to 20 minutes, or until tender when pierced. Drain and mash in a bowl with a potato masher or pass through a ricer or food mill into a bowl. Add the butter and stir until melted. Add the sour cream and, using an electric mixer or a large spoon, whip until smooth and fluffy. If necessary, thin with milk to the desired consistency. Stir in the 2 to 3 tablespoons of garlic blossom petals. Season with salt and white pepper. Keep warm.

Place the clarified butter in a shallow bowl and dip the salmon fillets, one at a time, into the butter. Place on the grill rack and grill, turning once, to the desired doneness. I recommend medium-rare if the fish is very fresh, which would be 3 to 5 minutes on each side, depending on the thickness of the fillets.

Mound an equal amount of the mashed potatoes on each of 4 individual serving plates. Top each mound with a salmon fillet and a few generous tablespoons of the crème fraîche mixture. Garnish with chive blossoms and caviar or chives, if desired. *Serves 4*

Vegetarian Shepherd's Pie with Potato and Leek Topping

This dish originated in England, where it remains a well-loved mainstay and a good way to use up bits of leftover meat and potatoes. This interpretation eliminates the traditional meat and uses a full-bodied onion mushroom stock to enhance the earthiness of the vegetables. Small shallots can be used in place of the pearl onions.

Pie Filling:

Ice water, to cover
1/2 basket pearl onions (15 to 25 onions), unpeeled
3/4 cup cubed carrots (1/2-inch cubes)
3/4 cup peeled and cubed parsnips or rutabagas
(1/2-inch cubes)
1 tablespoon light olive oil
1 cup sliced fresh domestic mushrooms
1/2 cup finely chopped spinach or Swiss chard
1/4 cup chopped mixed fresh tarragon, chives and
fennel tops, in any combination
1/4 cup Marsala wine
Salt and freshly ground black pepper, to taste
3/4 cup shelled peas (fresh or frozen, thawed)

Binding Sauce:

1/2 cup (1 stick) unsalted butter
1/2 cup unbleached white flour
2 cups Leek, Onion and Mushroom Stock
(recipe p. 65) or other vegetable stock
1/2 teaspoon salt
1/4 teaspoon white pepper
Dash of freshly grated nutmeg

Potato and Leek Topping:

2 pounds russet potatoes, peeled and cut into
large chunks
1/4 cup (1/2 stick) unsalted butter
2 large leeks, white part only, thinly sliced
1/2 cup sour cream
1 teaspoon salt
1/2 teaspoon white pepper
Milk, for thinning
Paprika

To make the pie base, fill a large pot three-fourths full of water and bring to a boil. Have ready a large bowl of ice water. Trim the root ends off the onions and drop the onions into the boiling water for a few minutes. Using a slotted spoon, transfer the onions to the ice bath. Reserve the boiling water in the pot. Peel the onions.

Return the onions to the same boiling water, along with the carrots and parsnips or rutabagas. Boil for approximately 5 minutes, or until tender when pierced.

At the same time, in a large sauté pan over medium heat, warm the olive oil. Add the mushrooms, spinach or chard and mixed herbs and sauté for approximately 5 minutes, or until the vegetables are soft.

Using the slotted spoon, retrieve the vegetables from the boiling water and add to the mushroom mixture in the pan. Reserve the water in the large pot. Add the Marsala to the mushroom mixture and toss all the ingredients together. Season generously with salt and pepper. Stir in the peas and remove from heat.

To make the binding sauce, in a medium-sized saucepan over medium heat, melt the butter. Whisk in the flour and cook, stirring constantly, for 3 or 4 minutes; do not allow the flour to brown. Gradually whisk in the stock and continue to cook, stirring, for approximately 5 minutes, or until thickened. Season

with salt, pepper and nutmeg. Add the mushroom mixture, stir well and transfer to a deep 2-quart baking dish.

Preheat the oven to 375 degrees F. To make the topping, bring the reserved vegetable cooking water to a boil. Add the potatoes and boil for approximately 15 minutes, or until tender when pierced. Drain and set aside in a large mixing bowl.

Meanwhile, in a sauté pan over medium heat, melt the butter. Add the leeks and sauté for approximately 10 minutes, or until very soft. Add the sautéed leeks to the potatoes, scraping any pan juices into the bowl as well. Add the sour cream, salt and pepper. By hand or with an electric mixer, beat the potatoes until smooth and fluffy, adding a little milk if necessary to achieve the proper consistency. Spread the potatoes over the seasoned vegetables. Sprinkle with the paprika.

Bake for approximately 1 hour, or until warmed throughout. Remove from the oven and let stand for 15 minutes. To serve, spoon into shallow bowls. *Serves 4 to 6*

Grilled Leeks and Radicchio over Hominy

I first made this dish on a cool winter's night. Rather than light the outdoor grill,
I placed the oil-coated leeks, just pulled from the garden, on a small grill built in the fireplace.
The aromas that filled the kitchen that night were as tantalizing as the leeks were delicious.
A garnish of rosemary aioli (recipe p. 61) goes nicely with this dish.

Ice water, to cover
12 small leeks
2 small heads radicchio
1/3 cup extra virgin olive oil
3 to 4 tablespoons balsamic vinegar
3 cloves garlic, minced
6 black peppercorns, crushed
1 tablespoon chopped fresh rosemary
1 1/2 teaspoons salt

Hominy:
2 tablespoons unsalted butter or olive oil
8 to 10 cloves garlic, thinly sliced
1/4 cup finely chopped sweet red bell pepper
1/4 cup finely chopped red onion
1/4 cup finely chopped carrot
1/4 cup chopped fresh parsley
2 cups drained, cooked whole hominy kernels
Salt and freshly ground black pepper, to taste

Prepare a charcoal fire so that the coals will be medium-hot in approximately 30 minutes.

Bring a medium-sized saucepan three-fourths full of water to a boil. Meanwhile, ready a bowl of ice water. Trim off the root ends, then cut or peel off any tough green leaves from the leeks, leaving only the white and tender light green portions. Rinse thoroughly.

Add the leeks to the boiling water and parboil for 3 to 5 minutes, or until slightly softened. Drain and immerse in ice water to chill well. Drain and pat dry with paper towels.

If large, cut the radicchio heads into quarters, with stems intact; if small, cut in half.

In a large bowl, stir together the olive oil, vinegar, garlic, peppercorns, rosemary and salt. Toss the leeks and radicchio in the mixture, coating all surfaces. Set aside.

To prepare the hominy, in a medium-sized sauté pan over medium heat, melt the butter or warm the oil. Add the garlic, bell pepper, red onion and carrot and sauté for 3 or 4 minutes, or until softened. Add the parsley and hominy and heat through. Season with salt and pepper. Cover and keep warm while you grill the leeks and radicchio.

Shake off any excess oil on the leeks and radicchio and arrange them on the grill rack and grill, turning often so that they don't burn, for approximately 15 minutes, or until nicely browned on all sides.

Serve the grilled vegetables atop the warm hominy mixture. *Serves 4*

Lamb Shanks and Shallots with Juniper Berry Sauce

A bouquet of shallots imparts a wonderful sweetness to this dish. Thyme-scented red lentils are a perfect partner.

6 lamb shanks (approximately 3/4 pound each)
Unbleached white flour, for dusting
Olive oil, for browning
18 shallots or pearl onions
1/2 pound fresh domestic button mushrooms or
    shiitake mushrooms, brushed clean and tough
    stems removed
2 carrots cut into 1-inch pieces
2 parsnips, peeled and cut into 1-inch pieces
5 cloves garlic, coarsely chopped

1 fennel bulb, coarsely chopped
1 large apple, peeled, cored and coarsely chopped
1 to 2 tablespoons bottled grated horseradish
1 tablespoon Worcestershire sauce
2 bay leaves
1 1/2 tablespoons juniper berries, coarsely crushed
1 1/2 cups full-bodied red wine
Meat stock or water, to cover
3 medium potatoes, peeled and quartered
Salt, to taste

Preheat the oven to 375 degrees F.

Dredge the lamb shanks in flour, coating them generously. In a large skillet over medium heat, warm enough oil to form a film on the pan bottom. Working in batches, add the lamb shanks and brown on all sides. Transfer to a large roasting pan. Add 12 of the shallots, the mushrooms, carrots, parsnips, garlic, fennel, apple, horseradish, Worcestershire sauce, bay leaves, juniper berries and wine to the roasting pan, distributing the ingredients evenly. Pour in stock to cover the shanks. Cover the pan and roast for 1 1/2 hours.

Add the potatoes and the remaining shallots and roast for 1 hour longer, or until the meat is soft and well done. It is better to overcook than undercook the shanks; ideally, the meat should be tender but still attached to the bone.

Remove from the oven, season with salt and let stand for 15 minutes. Serve one lamb shank per person, with juices and vegetables spooned alongside. *Serves 6*

Shallot Waffles with Creamed Pearl Onions and Turkey

*This recipe recalls the best of Southern cooking. It is the kind of dish you
want to eat at home, while sitting in front of the television set on a cold, rainy night.*

6 tablespoons (3/4 stick) butter
6 tablespoons unbleached white flour
2 1/3 cups milk or chicken stock
1 bay leaf
3/4 pound smoked turkey meat, shredded
2 tablespoons minced fresh parsley
3/4 basket pearl onions (15 to 25 onions)
1 large sweet potato, cooked, peeled and cut into
    bite-sized pieces
Salt and freshly ground black pepper, to taste

Shallot Waffles:
2 1/2 cups unbleached white flour
1 tablespoon granulated sugar
2 teaspoons baking powder
1/2 teaspoon salt
1/4 teaspoon freshly ground black pepper
1/4 cup (1/2 stick) unsalted butter
2 tablespoons chopped fresh sage
1/4 cup minced shallots
2 cups buttermilk
2 eggs

Chopped fresh chives or parsley, for garnish

To make the creamed turkey and onions, in a medium-sized saucepan over medium heat, melt the butter. Whisk in flour and cook, stirring constantly, for 3 to 4 minutes. Gradually whisk in milk or stock and add the bay leaf. Continue to cook, stirring occasionally, for approximately 5 minutes, or until thickened.

Cut off the root ends of the pearl onions, then boil them 5 to 8 minutes, or until tender. Drain and rinse under cold running water to cool, then peel off the skins. Add the cooked onions, parsley, smoked turkey and cooked sweet potato to the saucepan and stir well. Season with salt and pepper and keep warm over low heat while you make the waffles.

Preheat a waffle iron. While it heats, in a medium-sized bowl, stir together the flour, sugar, baking powder, salt and pepper. In a small sauté pan, melt the butter and add the sage and shallots. Sauté for approximately 5 minutes, or until softened. In another medium-sized bowl, whisk together the buttermilk and eggs and add the shallot mixture. Gradually beat the buttermilk mixture into the flour mixture.

Lightly brush the waffle iron with oil. Pour 3/4 cup of the batter (or the amount indicated by the manufacturer's instructions) onto the heated waffle iron. Bake the waffle until cooked through and lightly browned. Consult the manufacturer's instructions on when the waffle is ready. Transfer the waffle to a plate and keep warm while you cook the remaining waffles.

To serve, spoon a generous amount of the creamed mixture onto each waffle. Garnish with a sprinkling of parsley or chives. Serve immediately. *Serves 4 to 6*

Meat Loaf with Caramelized Onions

A good meat loaf is hard to beat, especially when smothered in caramelized onions and resting next to a mound of mashed potatoes and gravy. And for many of us, finding leftover meat loaf in the refrigerator to make a sandwich on white bread with catsup and onions brings back memories of Mom, home and great American food.

Meat Loaf:
1 pound ground beef
1 pound ground pork
3/4 cup finely chopped yellow onion (preferably fall/storage)
2 eggs
1/2 cup fine dried bread crumbs, or 2 slices bread, crusts removed and crumbled
1 teaspoon salt
1/2 teaspoon freshly ground black pepper

2 tablespoons chopped fresh sage
1 tablespoon Dijon mustard
1 tablespoon Worcestershire sauce
3/4 cup bottled chili sauce
3 slices bacon

Caramelized Onions:
2 tablespoons peanut oil
2 large yellow onions (preferably fall/storage), thinly sliced
Salt, to taste

Preheat the oven to 350 degrees F.

To make the meat loaf, in a large bowl, combine the beef, pork, onion, eggs, bread crumbs, salt, pepper, sage, mustard, Worcestershire sauce and 1/2 cup of the chili sauce. Mix together to combine thoroughly. Transfer to a large loaf pan. Spread the remaining 1/4 cup chili sauce evenly over the top and then cover with the bacon slices.

Bake for approximately 1 hour, or until an instant-read thermometer inserted into the center registers 170 degrees F., or the juices of the loaf run clear when it is pierced.

While the meat loaf is baking, prepare the caramelized onions. In a heavy-bottomed pan over medium heat, warm the peanut oil. Add the onions and sauté for approximately 45 minutes, or until they are soft and golden brown. Season with salt.

Remove the meat loaf from the oven and let stand for approximately 10 minutes. Drain off any fat. Run a thin-bladed knife around the edge of the pan to loosen, and then unmold onto a serving platter. Slice and serve with the caramelized onions or layer in between two slices of white bread. *Serves 6 to 8*

METRIC CONVERSIONS

Liquid Weights

U.S. Measurements	Metric Equivalents
1/4 teaspoon	1.23 ml
1/2 teaspoon	2.5 ml
3/4 teaspoon	3.7 ml
1 teaspoon	5 ml
1 dessertspoon	10 ml
1 tablespoon (3 teaspoons)	15 ml
2 tablespoons (1 ounce)	30 ml
1/4 cup	60 ml
1/3 cup	80 ml
1/2 cup	120 ml
2/3 cup	160 ml
3/4 cup	180 ml
1 cup (8 ounces)	240 ml
2 cups (1 pint)	480 ml
3 cups	720 ml
4 cups (1 quart)	1 litre
4 quarts (1 gallon)	3 3/4 litres

Dry Weights

U.S. Measurements	Metric Equivalents
1/4 ounce	7 grams
1/3 ounce	10 grams
1/2 ounce	14 grams
1 ounce	28 grams
1 1/2 ounces	42 grams
1 3/4 ounces	50 grams
2 ounces	57 grams
3 ounces	85 grams
3 1/2 ounces	100 grams
4 ounces (1/4 pound)	114 grams
6 ounces	170 grams
8 ounces (1/2 pound)	227 grams
9 ounces	250 grams
16 ounces (1 pound)	464 grams

Temperatures

Fahrenheit	Celsius (Centigrade)
32°F (water freezes)	0°C
200°F	95°C
212°F (water boils)	100°C
250°F	120°C
275°F	135°C
300°F (slow oven)	150°C
325°F	160°C
350°F (moderate oven)	175°C
375°F	190°C
400°F (hot oven)	205°C
425°F	220°C
450°F (very hot oven)	230°C
475°F	245°C
500°F (extremely hot oven)	260°C

Length

U.S. Measurements	Metric Equivalents
1/8 inch	3 mm
1/4 inch	6 mm
3/8 inch	1 cm
1/2 inch	1.2 cm
3/4 inch	2 cm
1 inch	2.5 cm
1 1/4 inches	3.1 cm
1 1/2 inches	3.7 cm
2 inches	5 cm
3 inches	7.5 cm
4 inches	10 cm
5 inches	12.5 cm

Approximate Equivalents

1 kilo is slightly more than 2 pounds

1 litre is slightly more than 1 quart

1 meter is slightly over 3 feet

1 centimeter is approximately 3/8 inch

INDEX